DEPRESSION PROOF
YOUR FUTURE

BY
ALGERNON HORATIO

AUTHOR OF
THE PENNY CAPITALIST

Process Books
Boulder, CO

Economic factors are subject to change on a daily basis. This book is not intended to provide specific recommendations for individual economic decisions. It provides guidance in assessing financial options and opportunities. For specific recommendations the reader should consult with financial advisors.

DEPRESSION PROOF YOUR FUTURE: A FINANCIAL GUIDE TO THE 21ST CENTURY

by Algernon Horatio (pseud.)

Copyright © 2003 by Hester Investment Trust

Process Books
4657 Huey Circle
Boulder, CO 80305

ISBN: 0-9710609-7-5

Library of Congress Control Number: 2002117011

Printed in the United States of America

0 9 8 7 6 5 4 3 2 1

To Wint who taught me all I know about depressions.

CONTENTS

Preface To The First Incarnation

When discussing the economy Alfred Kahn, the former President's Inflation Fighter, used the terms deep recession and depression. Immediately he was in public disgrace so he changed his term to banana. From that point on there was no recession in our future, only a "banana." Believe me, the depression, no matter what you call it, is coming; the question is not if, but when. Will you be prepared? Even if what confronts us is termed a "deep recession" remember the difference between that and a "depression" is only three letters, so now is the time for you to prepare for that eventuality. What follows is not a gloomsday book, predicting disaster in moralistic tones. It is a how to do it manual to prepare you for the tough times that lie ahead.

If you are worried about your financial future and fit the following profile then this book is for you.

Age—25-55

Dependents—several

Income—over committed

Debts—3 times annual salary

Non-job-related income—minimal

Expensive hobbies—several

Total tax deductions—minimal

If job lost—in financial difficulty within 30 days

Consumable items—buy everything in the store

Major assets—primarily the equity on your home

Savings, cash, and short-term certificates—minimal

Freedom to change jobs or move—limited

   If you fit most of the above categories then you have a problem, since you are in a vulnerable position and could not survive a depression without major deprivation. The purpose of this book is to alert you to the nature of depressions, their causes, and to provide pragmatic advice as to how you may prepare now so that you will be able to survive the difficult times that lie ahead.

PREFACE TO THE SECOND INCARNATION

This manuscript was originally written in 1980. The theme was simple, in the good times you should prepare for the bad times. I obtained a book agent and he shuffled the manuscript back and forth to publishers. None chose to publish it since times were good, the economy was booming, and the good times were expected to go on forever.* Let the good times roll *(le bonton roleil)*. "The economic cycle has been repealed." This was a new economy and it could only go up. And that's what happened right through the 1980's and 90's. Then suddenly, in the year 2000, the economy reversed itself. We had the Dot Com crash; the roller coaster was going downhill. At that point the question became, Is there anything in that prior manuscript that is still relevant? Is it too late for that advice to be applied? Reviewing the manuscript I determined that much of it is still relevant. So here it is, revised to meet the conditions of the 21st century.

---

* The same thing was experienced by John Kenneth Galbraith (1990, p. 8). In the fall of 1986 he wrote that a speculative euphoria existed and that a market crash was inevitable. Even though the editors of the New York Times had solicited the article, they refused to publish it. In the good times no one wants to hear that they are about to end. Nonetheless, on schedule as Galbraith had predicted, the crash came in October, 1987.

PART I

HOW IT IS

CHAPTER 1
GEORGE AND YOU

E very morning I catch the bus and then the subway on the way to the office. I don't mind commuting since it gives me time to arrange my thoughts and to read. Others read along the way as well; about half read and of those 40% are currently reading the latest best seller, 40% the morning daily, and one or two the *Wall Street Journal.*

As I look over the reader's shoulder the best seller has sentences like, "I crushed her to me tenderly, she cried; muffled into my shoulder, 'Oh hold me, I need you,'" etc. Meanwhile what am I reading? Things like Galbraith's *Crash of '29,* Erdman's *Crash of '79, Only Yesterday, How to Profit in the Monetary Crisis,* and other such froth. In fact, during the boom of the 90's with at least 1,000 people on the train, I'm probably the only one reading about monetary crashes and the Great Depression. Why am I doing so and what does it bode for you? The reason is that George—your friend and mine—has a severe case of anemia. George, of course, is the familiar face on the dollar bill and these days he's peering out rather plaintively as everyone is taking his pulse and finding it lacking.

Traditionally a nation's currency has served two major functions, as a medium of exchange and as a repository of value. In his famous message dated August 1971, President Nixon stated the devaluation of the U.S. currency would cause little effect on the average U.S. citizen. Little did he know how incredibly wrong he could be and few of the citizens knew either. Today we know that the dollar won't buy much on that European vacation; for example, it takes $5.00 to buy a cup of coffee. We also know that the the price of imported cars and other goods has gone up dramatically but prices on goods manufactured at home have gone up too—so what's the difference? The difference is that the dollar isn't worth anything anymore, or at least it is only worth whatever someone will give for it.

The dollar per se, is nothing more than a piece of paper with some ink on it. It has no intrinsic worth since the government no longer agrees to exchange it upon demand for anything else of value. The only value now ascribed to the dollar is given by you, the average citizen, in your willingness to accept it in exchange for goods or work performed. International currency traders are also willing to exchange pounds, or francs, lira or yen for the good old greenback, but at continually reducing rates. Some days recently the dollar has lost 1% of its ascribed value. The government says that they will support it by selling gold or wheat or by buying dollars in the open market with other currencies held. However, none of these maneuvers has any staying power so soon the dollar sells off again.

What are the underlying causes of this dilemma and how will it affect your future?

Part of the problem is the direct result of the fourfold increase in the world price of oil engineered by the OPEC nations. We need the oil—we can't get along without it—and we cannot rapidly replace it with other sources of energy. Therefore, it has become the unstated policy of our government that imported oil will be paid for by simply printing more money. No matter that any increase in the money supply cheapens the value of every other dollar in circulation. What counts is that as long as the Arabs are willing to accept paper dollars for oil, we get the oil for free. For free? Well, not really, since depreciation of the dollar affects everyone who has any money in the bank, or funds in an interest bearing account, or in a pension plan. In short, the headlong printing of money today is mortgaging your future since it reduces the value of much of what you have laid by for a rainy day.

The effects of such a policy are two-fold: It is a form of hidden taxation, since it steals from the thrifty without their knowledge, and secondly, and more importantly, it has destroyed the function of our currency as a repository of value. No one can knowingly permit his resources to be kept in dollars. All currency received must be converted as soon as possible into some form of real wealth such as marks, francs, yen, gold, silver, diamonds, antiques, or real estate. Only in that fashion can one's assets be kept insured against erosion of buying power. In short, our currency is now only a medium of exchange—useful only to spend not to save.

Why is the currency of other nations a repository of wealth while ours is not? There are two reasons: The exports of such a nation exceed the value of its imports—in other words, it has a positive balance of trade, and/or it has a currency backed by items of real wealth, gold or silver. The latter constitute real wealth since they have been historically recognized as useful, nice to own, and have a known degree of rarity. It is not possible to manipulate increases in the mining of precious metals in the same manner as printing paper currency. Precious metals are precious because they are rare and the demand exceeds the supply. Furthermore, they have been recognized for their intrinsic value since the invention of coinage more than 2,000 years ago.

The monetary policy boys at the Treasury say that we don't need that barbaric legacy of gold anymore. We can back our currency with the good old U.S. production; our GNP(Gross National Product) is the strongest in the world; key the dollar to production and we no longer need Ft. Knox. They are right, in fact, as long as production is high and exports exceed imports. What is wrong in the equation is our need for imported oil, we are like junkies addicted to oil, and we will pay any price, because we have to have it. Without a sure cure, which would require massive production of new domestic oil, we are like a hemophiliac who, once cut, keeps on bleeding. Our loss is not blood but the financial wealth of the nation and at this point in time the end of the trend is not in sight.

Now we must go back to a fundamental consideration for a moment. What is a dollar really worth today, or perhaps more understandable, how much of the buying power of the dollar has been lost in recent years? Newspaper articles, citing as source the

Department of Labor, illustrated the U.S. dollar, with the faces of our presidents on each, as worth the following during their presidencies: Eisenhower, 1958—$1.00; Kennedy, 1963—94 cents; Johnson, 1968—83 cents; Nixon, 1973—64 cents; and Carter, 1978—44 cents. If we are to believe this rate of diminution, the dollar lost 66% of its purchasing power over those 20 years or 3.3% per year, continuing that rate to today, the dollar is now worth 12 cents. I guess at this point you may be somewhat skeptical since the announced rate of inflation since 1970 has been 3% per year. Meanwhile, it is fair to ask how is this residual purchasing power computed? Purchasing of "what" is the key question. It is likely that such computations take into account only the increase in the cost of domestically produced items whose market price is in one way or another *regulated* by actions of the government. If we consider other commodities—which do not have any federal control—we perceive an entirely different picture. Since 1958 the price of gold has increased from $35.00 to $300.00 per ounce—an increase of 850%. The price of silver has increased from $1.29 to $4.50 per ounce—an increase of 735%. If we average the increases to obtain a precious metal index, that index has increased in value relative to the dollar by 800%. Similarly, you know and I know that the price of imported cars has doubled over the past 5 years or approximately 20% per year, hospital costs are up 16.5% over the last year, etc. With this additional information we can now assign real values to the two aspects of our currency—as a medium of exchange, and as a repository of value. As a medium of exchange, used in the purchase of currently produced domestic items, the dollar has retained one eighth of its 1958 buying power. However in the purchase of any items of lasting value, such as gold, silver, real estate, antiques, fine art, classic automobiles, gemstones, and goods imported from abroad including oil, the dollar has retained 5% to 10% of its 1958 buying power. Therefore, we can clearly perceive the fundamental distinction between these two aspects of our currency. We can label them the inflation dollar and the real dollar. Has your salary increased 800% since 1958? If not, then you have lost purchasing power in terms of real wealth. Have your investments increased in dollar value by 800% since 1958? If not, then you have lost ground in the struggle to achieve financial security.

Now that you understand the above distinction you can perceive that the rate of interest paid on funds you invested is returned to you in inflation dollars. Meanwhile the savings and loan company loaned out your funds to a home buyer who used them to buy property which increased in value in real dollars at a rate of 10% or more per year.

After taxes, brokerage commissions, and inflation, the rate of return on funds invested over the last decade in interest bearing accounts and securities, may in fact be negative. Meanwhile, the smart investor who has immediately exchanged his inflation dollars for equities has seen his real wealth increase rapidly. This is true, notwithstanding the downturn in the stock market beginning in 2000.

How long will this situation continue and what does it portend for your financial future?

If this trend continues the future will be marked by dramatic events. We will see continuing inflation in the prices of goods and services but, in addition, we will perceive runaway inflation in the prices of things of real value. Failures of major financial institutions becomes an increasingly logical possibility. When this occurs, businesses can no longer obtain funds they need to conduct or expand their capacity for conducting business. Such a pinch on the financial front will be translated into reductions in production and reductions in the work force. With more and more people out of work, fewer will have the resources to buy the goods being produced, which further increases the depth of the depressionary spiral. A full-fledged depression once underway is very difficult to reverse owing to the self-contributing aspects of all of its interrelated aspects.

Can such a depression, like that beginning in 1929, happen here again? You betcha! Will it happen soon? Such as next year or the year after? Possibly.

Almost certainly it will happen unless our government takes drastic remedial action. What kind of actions would avert such a cataclysmic sequence of future events?

Harry Schultz reviewed these problems in 1972 and recommended the following list of economic solutions (Schultz 1972, p.

195). What is interesting is to review his recommendations years later and see how few have been adopted. His list included:

1.   Drastic tax cutting.*

2.   Slashing of government spending.

3.   Re-pricing of gold upward by 200%**

4.   Restore backing and convertibility to currency.

5.   Discontinue subsidies to farmers and businessmen.

6.   Remove currency controls.

7.   Legalize gold ownership.**

Whereas all of the above recommendations would seem to lie within the capability of our government, I sincerely doubt that many will be implemented since they would have detrimental side effects including a business recession, tightening of consumer credit, and a rise in unemployment. These potential ills are politically unpalatable. Whether they will come to be viewed as bitter medicine, which must be taken to cure the disease, is yet to be determined.

Meanwhile, what are the chances that my prognosis is wrong? Can we continue indefinitely with an economy managed to a fine degree by the federal establishment in such a manner that we will have an "acceptable" level of inflation and a continuing era of national prosperity? I hope so, however, in general, the indicators appear to be negative.

As we have stated above, everyone knows about these problems. Furthermore, everyone is anxious about their ability to meet rising costs of living and to provide for a secure financial future and retirement. We can gain little comfort from our government or its leaders as too often their solutions and their predictions of future events are proven to be dramatically wrong only a few months after they are unveiled. Does anyone know what is wrong or what the future course of events will be? Is it possible to predict the future or is it simply a futile exercise? Of course no one knows for sure, but one man has been more accurate than anyone else.

(* accomplished in 2001)
(** accomplished by 1979)

His name is Donald J. Hoppe and in 1970 he wrote an amazingly accurate forecast of the events to come. I have added dates to provide a correlation between his forecast and the actual march of events. Some of the events he predicts are yet to come. It is the purpose of this book to help you prepare to meet them.

Year in which Hoppe's prediction actually occurred:

1970   1. Accelerating inflation: galloping price increases, massive labor unrest, crippling strikes, impossible wage settlements, staggering property tax increases.

1971   2. Wholesale worldwide devaluations, with the pound, the franc, and the lira leading the way

1971   3. U.S. embargo on gold exports and refusal of all further redemptions of central bank dollar holdings. Result: de facto devaluation of U.S. dollar in world markets.

1974   4. U.S. action leads to: gradual worldwide abandonment of convertibility; floating exchange rates, wide fluctuations in the market price of gold; removal of all restrictions of private gold dealings. Gold demonetization in the U.S. and Great Britain.

1978   5. Collapse and breakup of the IMF; beginning of a new European Common Market gold-backed reserve currency. As of today, 2002, we have the Euro but it is not yet backed by gold.

1971-73

Wage-price controls imposed by Nixon

6. Stringent economic restrictions imposed by the U.S.; "tight money" policies resumed; partial wage and price controls begun; prime interest rates reach 10 to 15 percent.

1974-75

Worst recession since the 1930's

7. Severe business depression begins in the U.S.; drastic declines in employment, stock prices, real estate, etc; massive social unrest.

1975-78   8. Panic resumption of federal deficit spending and lending, resulting in huge budget deficits—perhaps as high as $40 to $50 billion in the first year.

Oct. 1978

U.S. Government begins sale of foreign denominated bonds and gold

9. Foreign gold bonds and gold-guaranteed private debt issues appear; regular bonds and notes selling at deep discounts or are virtually unsalable.

1979   10. Only partial recovery from depression, but inflation resumes in earnest; paradoxically purchasing power of paper dollar declines rapidly in the midst of general economic stagnation. Crime and disorder in major cities at times almost unbearable.

Contemplated in 1979 are gas rationing and wage and price controls.

11. U.S. government adopts a new authoritarian economic and social policies: severe wage and price controls enforced; national police force established to assist local authorities in maintaining order and combating crime; permissive social attitudes strongly rejected by public.

Yet to come

12. U.S. government announces new gold policy; building of national gold reserve given first priority; all privately owned gold bullion ordered to be surrendered to Treasury at fixed price under pain of severe penalty for evasion; all gold in U.S. nationalized again (except for gold coins of recognized numismatic value); mining activity greatly stimulated by an increasing Treasury gold price, and by special grants for exploration, recovery etc. Exports to gold-rich countries, such as Canada, South Africa encouraged by special subsidies and government assistance.

Yet to come

13. National gold reserve greatly expanded; Currency stabilized by a return to fixed parity with gold. "New Dollar"

established—old dollars exchanged at 10 to 1, 100 to 1, or who knows what, with new dollars.

Yet to come

Great international monetary meeting to establish a new system of fixed exchange rates among major trading nations.

Yet to come

New era of international monetary cooperation begins, domestic economic restrictions eased; general prosperity resumes.

Hoppe claims that he is no psychic. However his predictions have come true with an amazing degree of accuracy and pretty much in the order that they were presented. The only major differences between his forecast and reality are two: 1. He did not anticipate the energy crunch, and 2. His time schedule was too rapid. After many years have elapsed we still look forward to considerable social and financial unrest prior to the reestablishment of a sound U.S. financial policy based on gold. Viewed in this context, Hoppe's predictions were no accident. They were and are based on sound economic cause and effect relationships. In other words, if A occurs then B will follow. If we accept this line of reasoning then it follows that the seeming inability of our government to control inflation, the national debt, negative balance of payments, and unemployment is due to one or more of the following reasons:

1.   Our politicians are too dumb to understand their economic advisors.

2.   Their economic advisors are too dumb to understand economics.

3.   Both the politicians and their advisors know the score and they are

        a. Lying to us and

        b. Are afraid to take the proper actions to solve the problems and are only willing to deal with the symptoms in an image-enhancing manner.

Obviously this explanation is too simplistic, however, as we will see later on, many of the governmental actions taken to "cope" with these major economic problems can be explained by 3a and 3b above.

So far we have briefly reviewed the current problems and their relationship to the march of events as forecast by Donald Hoppe. In the chapters to come we will review how similar situations in the past affected people's fortunes and daily lives. We will then examine the problems we face today to permit a clearer view of what we may expect in the future. Finally, in Part IV we will offer advice as to how to deal with the difficult times ahead.

Australian aborigines speak of the time before the present as "The Dreamtime". This is what we experienced in the 1990's. The 90's were a time out of step with reality. The dot com boom led to incredible excesses, instant fortunes derived from stock options extending down the corporate pyramid even to receptionists and stockroom clerks. Every working professional expected to retire a millionaire with the stock profits in his or her 401K plan. The dramatic crash in the market beginning in 2000 has ended those unrealistic expectations. The future we have to deal with in the 21st century will again be based on reality.

A Warning

The most difficult part about this entire book is convincing you, the reader, that these are not ordinary times. Strange as it may seem, the major problems you will face in the near future are not coping with inflation or facing long gas lines. The day-to-day fight against higher and higher prices, difficult as that may be, is not the principal problem you will face. The really tough one coming up is the possibility of a total financial collapse, not only within the U.S. but worldwide. The U.S. has successfully exported inflation through its profligate printing of money. The use of the dollar as a worldwide medium of exchange has led every nation to accept this overvalued currency. Like a rotten apple in a barrel, the disease has spread to affect every currency in the world. Even West Germany and Switzerland, long the bastions of hard currency, are now experiencing their bouts of inflation. If we can convince you that a total monetary collapse is a very real possibility then you will begin to see how difficult the future may be.

Between now and then we will go through a recession, followed (in my opinion) by a return to galloping inflation. If that inflation should really take off to 20% per year or more it may well be impossible to keep things under control. From that moment on the possibility of a total monetary collapse becomes very real indeed. To avoid such a collapse at that point we would have to have both a strong intelligent economically sophisticated national administration coupled with an electorate equally determined to bring inflation under control. At present neither of these requirements seems likely to occur.

The point that I wish to make is that given our current need for an adequate energy supply, coupled with the deficit spending required by a wide range of federal programs, plus union demands for inflation, with a concurrent tax revolt in progress, and facing international pressure on the dollar, our government has few courses of action left available to cope with the situation. The laws of economics will prevail, the business cycle will reassert itself and the direction of that cycle is down since we have had almost total prosperity since the beginning of World War II. However, in the 60's and '70's that prosperity was achieved as a result of greater and greater infusions of fiat currency. It is a self-feeding monster, and if our historical examples may be given credence then the only possible future course of action is runaway inflation followed by a collapse, followed by a depression. Another possible scenario would be runaway inflation followed by a monetary reorganization with each new dollar worth 20 or some other multiple of the old dollars. What we can call the Argentinean solution. Such a plan might or might not be coupled with a return to a gold backed currency. If not, then the "new" dollars would soon begin depreciating and we would have a return to runaway inflation again.

What I am trying to communicate is that in spite of whatever our governmental officials may say, or whom they may blame, the situation is very, very serious. In fact it is out of control. And the future is going to be very difficult indeed.

PART II

HOW IT WAS— SPECULATIVE BOOMS OF THE PAST

CHAPTER 2
HISTORICAL PRECEDENTS

The purpose of our historical review is to bring to your attention past times of economic crisis. These crises will be described in terms of what happened, what were the causal factors, and what were the long-term economic and social effects. What we have to combat is the widespread opinion that today's cause and effect relationships are different from those in the past. Such complacency was also common in the past and led to national leaders affirming that "prosperity is here forever" and "we have eliminated the economic cycle." My major purpose then in this historical section is to refresh your memory and in addition to stimulate your paranoia to the point where you may concede that such unfortunate events could happen again. Not all of our examples are from the 20th century either. They include the period between the French Revolution and the rise of Napoleon as well as happenings in Ancient Rome. It is easy to see what went wrong in our historical examples since we can see how it all ended.

What is more difficult is to identify in advance of catastrophic event the things that were going wrong that led up to it. Yet that is our final assignment. Think how much better off you would be today if your parents or grandparents had been warned that the depression was coming and could have prepared for it in time!

Lessons From the Coin Collectors

The history of money begins with coinage. The earliest forms, such as the Egyptian ring money, did not embody the distinctive characteristics of coins which serve to guarantee the principles of true money. These principles are that the money is of a standard weight and purity with a recognized value certified by the state. These attributes guarantee that the money will be both acceptable as a medium of exchange and as a repository of value. I shall not attempt here a history of money and coinage since that is a major topic in itself and has already been covered in detail by numerous numismatists and historians. However the cessation of coinage of U.S. coins in silver in 1965, the recall of silver certificates, and the removal of gold backing to our currency in 1971 lead us to study similar historical precedents. From earliest times coins were subjected to a variety of vicissitudes. Their weight and purity were changed, their edges were clipped, they were abraded, and they were officially debased with the new coinage having a stated value greater than their intrinsic value. All of these official governmental actions led to inflation, further debasement of the coinage, and eventually the stockpiling of coins into hoards, the return of the barter system for essentials, and finally a reorganization of the coinage at some new standard. Such events have repeatedly transpired in the past and the pattern is ever the same. It is sufficient here to review one such episode in detail from the Roman Empire (Porteous 1969, pp. 8-14).

> The origins of modern coinage are deeply rooted in the monetary system of the Roman Empire. The emperor Augustus issued coins in gold, silver and copper. The centrepiece of his system was the silver denarius in terms of which most prices were quoted and the army and civil service were paid. The gold aureus was effectively coined bullion, its value unfixed in fixed fractions of the denarius, their values artificially supported by imperial control of metal prices. The superior pieces were made of brass, the inferior of pure copper ... The economy of the Roman Empire was subject to a growing burden of defense and administrative costs, unmatched by any increase in production. The deficit was met partly by higher

taxes and partly by inflation which took the simple form of debasement of the *denarius*. For about two hundred years this debasement proceeded at a supportable pace, though even then it was enough to leave some of the silver currencies of the eastern empire high and dry, and they disappeared during that time. In the third century the process began to get out of hand as military pressure built up on the frontiers and political disintegration within compelled successive emperors to bid more and more for the army's support. The denarius contained about 40% silver* when in 214 Caracalla replaced it as the standard coin by a double *denarius* intrinsically worth only about one and a half of the current pieces. During the next fifty years matters went from bad to worse. The double *denarius* became virtually a copper coin with the merest wash of silver which soon wore off° . . . The government tried to avoid the consequences of its own acts by insisting on payment of taxes in bullion and refusing to take its own coin, but that only made matters worse. Finally, in the wake of Valerian's defeat and the capture in 260 by the Sassanian King Shapur, the emperor Gallienus abandoned all restraint in striking the new wholly debased double denarius. Enormous numbers were issued, the government's credit was destroyed and the currency became worthless.

The inflation of Gallienus' reign was almost as intense as that of Germany in 1923 and far more widespread. Nevertheless it may not have been so grievous in its social effects. The Roman Empire was never a monetary economy in the modern sense. Nearly all wealth was held in the form of land; agriculture was by far the most important economic activity. There was little manufacturing

---

*Just like the U.S. minting of 40% silver coins in 1965.

°Analogous to our current copper-nickle sandwich coins.

industry and most of that was owned and operated by the imperial government. The class which
might have accumulated savings was small. The
enormous hoards of double *denarii* dating from
Gallienus' reign suggest not so much savings lost
in the crash as the abandoned hopes of currency
speculators. It is more likely that the crisis caused
on overall drop in the standard of living than that
it ruined whole sections of the population. Money
ceased to be the prime medium of exchange. Payment of taxes, the remuneration of the civil service
and the army, all came to be made in kind. For
the taxpayers this meant an increase in the levy to
cover the cost of storage, wastage and transport
of commodities. On the other hand no number
of rations *(annonae)* were likely to compensate
such officials as provincial governors for the high
monetary salaries which they had enjoyed in former times. Private soldiers ceased to receive any
regular pay; they merely got their keep. As for the
peasants, the collapse of the currency, by impairing
the market for their occasional surpluses, simply
brought them nearer than ever to subsistence
level . . .

Whatever the distress caused to the population by the monetary disorder, the soldier emperors who succeeded Gallienus gave low priority to
finding a remedy for it. . . .

It was not until 295-6 that reform of the currency was firmly taken in hand by the emperor
Diocletian as part of a general renewal of the civil
institutions of the empire. Diocletian's reform of
the currency is still imperfectly understood, for
there are no documemts to explain it and the coins
themselves are enigmatic, but some facts about it
stand out clearly.

The Alexandrian *tetradrachm*, last survivor of
Greek coinage within the empire, was discontin-
ued, thus leaving the field absolutely clear for the

new coinage. New mints were set up to provide one in theory for each of the dioceses or super-provinces into which Diocletian divided the empire. The practice of marking every coin with the mint name and code number of the issuing officina or mint workshop was extended to become a general rule. The mints were thus decentralized and yet made easily subject to central supervision, an arrangement typical of Diocletian's administrative reforms.

As regards the coinage itself, Diocletian's most important change was to make his system revolve round the gold coin. The aureus had not been discredited like the denarius. During the third century it had become rare and had tended to fluctuate somewhat in weight; but it was never to the emperor's advantage to debase it since his own liabilities were rarely expressed in terms of it, whereas obligations to him were often paid that way. It was therefore the one piece which was still worth having. Diocletian stabilized its weight at sixty to the Roman pound and issued it in larger quantities. At the same time he issued a silver coin at ninety-six to the Roman pound, struck very pure and marked with the figures XCVI to encourage public confidence in it.

The gold and silver coinage is the good side of Diocletian's reform. His failure, and it was fundamental, was that he did not fix the rate of exchange between the gold and silver on one hand and the bronze on the other. . . .

In its details, so far as they can be assessed, Diocletian's coinage was short-lived. The weight of the follis and of the other bronze coins was continually changing. The silver coin with its mark of value was never reissued in precisely the same form. Finally in 312 Constantine the Great found it convenient to adjust the weight of the gold coin from sixty to seventy-two to the pound. He called

the new coin solidus, signifying perhaps by the
name his intention of consolidating and stabiliz-
ing the coinage on the basis of this new weight
standard. . . .

If any of this sounds familiar it is because the desires of
government are ever to profit monetarily at the expense of the
people while simultaneously refusing to acknowledge the damage
their actions cause in the inflation of currency, decrease in the
standard of living, and the eventual breakdown in the system of
exchange and the economy. Their efforts to revalue and stabilize
the currency are also, often, only the prelude to a further round
of inflation, with money chasing scarce goods, hoarding, a return
to barter followed by the eventual reorganization of the currency
again. Think how the Roman example is similar to the debasement
of our own current money. First in 1965 the U.S. stopped minting 90% silver coins. These were replaced with 40% silver coins.
These were then replaced with the copper-nickle sandwich coins
that Harry Brown calls "tokens." Now even the tokens are debased
with the Susan B. Anthony dollar being of smaller size than the
Kennedy half dollar, and the Sacajawea dollar quarter sized. Now
does the Roman example seem so far away and irrelevant?

We will now consult a more recent example taken from
studies of the coin collectors. Few Americans, other than coin
collectors, know the history of our own coinage. The Articles of
Confederation adopted in 1777 gave the United States through
Congress the sole right to establish the alloy and value of coins
struck under their authority (Schilke and Solomon 1964, p. 17).
This power was later incorporated within the Constitution. The
dollar was then defined by Congress on August 8, 1786 as a coin
containing 375.64 grains of fine silver (Schilke and Solomon 1964,
p. 15). Minting of the U.S. dollar was authorized under the Coinage Act of 1792 and the U.S. Mint was established with the actual
minting of coins beginning in 1793 (Schilke and Solomon 1964,
p. 20). What few Americans know today is that foreign coins of
gold and silver circulated in the United States as legal tender side
by side with U.S. coins until that practice was ended by congress
in 1857. Congress authorized the mint to assay foreign coins of
silver and gold to specify at what exchange rates they were to be
accepted as legal tender. The reason that foreign coins were legally
usable for the conduct of business and the settlement of debts was

the U.S. minted coins were in short supply. This situation, which lasted for 64 years, was directly due to the fact that the coins were money. The coins were the store of value and the government's supply of bullion was too limited to meet the demand. Instead of relying on an inflationary policy of issuing quantities of currency without backing, the government solved its need for currency by relying on foreign coins. This example points out the fact that when a government issue *is* money that issue is in *limited quantity* since true wealth is an asset in *limited supply* and *always has been.* Our currency government's flight from real money to a fiat currency backed by nothing, is the opposite course of action. Historically, from Roman times to the present, all such debasement of a government's money has led to bankruptcy. In addition to the threat of future bankruptcy of the nation, the current unbacked currency makes it impossible to conduct business in an orderly fashion since the value of the dollar changes on a daily basis!

The French Connection

In our search for historic parallels the period of the French Revolution affords another clear cut case of hyperinflation and its consequences. Described in detail more than a century ago by Andrew Dickson White, his review has recently been republished (White 1979). We will quote brief portions of his essay here but our primary goal is to seek to isolate the causal factors in the French inflationary binge and to relate them to our current situation.

> Early in the year 1789, the French nation found itself in deep financial embarrassment: there was a heavy debt and a serious deficit. The vast reforms of that period, though a lasting blessing politically, were a temporary evil financially. There was a general want of confidence in business circles; capital had shown its proverbial timidity by retiring out of sight as far as possible; throughout the land was stagnation . . .

> There was a general search for some short road to prosperity: the idea was soon set afloat that the great want of the country was more of the circulating medium; and this was speedily followed by calls for an issue of paper money. (White 1979, p.40).

That public debate led to the issuance of a paper currency, termed assignats, secured by land confiscated from the church. The concept was that issuance of the assignats would increase business activity and lead to prosperity. Initially these goals seemed to be achieved, part of the public debt was paid off, credit was stimulated and business increased. However soon these funds had all been spent and the government was again in distress. The outcry to print more assignats began. A chronology of the events that followed, both political and financial, is set out on the following pages.

Chronology

Assignats in

Circulation (millions

of livres or francs)

1793

January 31	More *assignats*	3,000
Feb.-March	Formation of Committee of Public Safety; rioting in Paris over high prices; Revolutionary Tribunal established; Reign of Terror begins.	
May 3	Price control on grains.	
June 22	Forced loan decreed— a progressive income tax.	
August 1	Trading in specie prohibited.	
Sept. 29	Law of the Maximum— price control extended to all food.	
Oct. 16	Marie Antoinette beheaded. Over 3,000 million new *assignats* issued during the year of which 1,200 million entered circulation.	4,200

1794

June 4	Robespierre elected president of National Convention; thousands executed by decree of Revolutionary Tribunal.	
July 27	Robespierre beheaded; end of Reign of Terror.	
December	*Assignats* in circulation at end of year.	7,000

1795

May 31	More rioting; business and trade Disrupted; shorages persist; uncertain government.	
July 31	*Assignats* in circulation.	14,000
Sept. 23	New Constitution adopted and new government formed— The Directory.	35,000

1796

Feb. 18	Machinery, plates, and paper for Printing assignats destroyed. First issue of new paper notes *mandats*— to displace *assignats* at 30:1.	40,000
August	*Mandats* worth only 3% of face value About 2,500 million mandats issued.	

1797

Feb.	Legal tender qualities withdrawn from both *assignats* and *mandats,* which became worthless after May.

1799

November 10	Napoleon comes into power -"to save the Republic."

(White 1979, pp. 56-58)

Two facts emerge from the French example. The first is that the expected results of increased business activity, etc., did occur as predicted after each issue of new assignats. However the problem was that soon after the former problems returned, credit dried up, business activity lagged, and the government was again unable to meet its expenses. The second fact was that each new issue was larger than the previous. In other words each time it took a larger bucket to bail out the boat. Other associated aspects are summed in this quote from the historian Van Sybel (White 1979, pp. 56-57):

> Before the end of the year 1795, the paper money was almost exclusively in the hands of the working classes, employees and men of small means, whose property was not large enough to invest in stores or goods or national lands. Financiers and men of large means were shrewd enough to put as much of their property as possible into objects of permanent value. The working classes had no such foresight, skill, or means. On them finally came the great crushing weight of the loss. After the first collapse came up the cries of the starving. Roads and bridges were neglected; many manufacturers were given up in utter helplessness ... None felt any confidence in the future in any respect; few dared to make a business investment for any length of time, and it was accounted a folly to curtail the pleasures of the moment, to accumulate or save for so uncertain a future.

Does that sound familiar? At the beginning of this era an unskilled worker earned one livre (the equivalent of the later franc) per day of which about half went for bread, sixty percent of his daily diet. Seven years later the price of bread had risen to 80 francs in currency and shortly thereafter was no longer available except for gold or silver coin. By the end, in 1796, there had been placed in circulation more than 40 billion francs in paper money and the exchange with gold stood at one gold franc for 600 paper francs. The end came with the destruction of the printing presses and an eventual return to hard money with the issuance of the silver Napoleons. In the meantime gamblers and speculators had become millionaires while the working classes lost all they had. The relevance of the French example to our current situation is there for all to see. The wholesale printing of paper money enriches a few at the expense of the majority. In a recent column Ellen Goodman stated:

> Inflation devastates our attempts to control our futures—to budget and predict and expect. It particularly makes fools out of people who saved then to buy now...it isn't fair if those who work and save, plan and postpone aren't given a better shake. We want the winners to be deserving...To a certain extent it rewards instant gratification and makes a joke out of our traditional notions of preparation.

What is frightening to us today is that is the same thing that Van Sybel said in the 1790's.

The Runaway Inflation of 1923

Germany, after World War I experienced the greatest episode of runaway inflation in the entire 20th century (Fig. 1). The basic cause of the inflation was the war debts to be paid by Germany as stipulated in the Treaty of Versailles. Since these payments exceeded the ability of the German nation to repay, the stimulus for inflation was created. By 1920 prices had increased 500% above the 1918 levels. During 1921 the increase in prices was limited to only 40% but by 1922 prices had gained a second 500%. In the last year of runaway inflation prices increased an incredible 14,000% (Schultz 1972, p. 101). By the end, in 1924, when it took a wheelbarrow load of currency to buy a loaf of bread, the new mark was established at one gold mark to one trillion of the paper marks! This inflationary episode was ended in a *single* day by the resolve to revalue the currency to give it a fixed value tied to an index commodity of world wide recognized value—gold.

1. Several major characteristics are notable in the 1923 inflationary debacle:

2. People spent their currency as fast as possible to buy goods before the prices went up again.

3. Prices went up daily and even hourly but few people were profiting since they could not replace their stock as cheaply as they had just sold it.

3.   Wages did not keep up with the prices therefore output and incentive decreased.

4.   There was an increase in unproductive workers. In many cases their time was spent in accounting and in labor disputes—both direct results of the inflation.

5.   With the emphasis on prices, businessmen devoted their energies to hoarding and buying and selling on the foreign markets in order to wedge out a profit through arbitrage. Consequently, there was a decrease in quality and quantity of domestically produced items.

6.   Caught up in the wage/price squeeze, the assets of the middle class were wiped out.

7.   Debtors engaged in a form of financial tag. They chased their creditors and whenever they caught them they forced payment of their debts in the worthless currency.

8.   The social chaos that resulted lasted a decade and paved the way to power for Adolph Hitler.

9.   The stock market did not keep up with the increase in prices, therefore it did not prove to be a hedge against the inflation (Fig. 1). Those who held stocks throughout the inflation lost 75% of their original capital (Schultz 1972, p. 106).

10.   After the devaluation mortgage debt was established at 15% of its original capital value. Thus lenders (those who retained their ownership) lost 85% of their original capital assets (Schultz 1972, p. 106). Even at that discount the consequences of paying for the hyperinflation caused the bankruptcy rate to rise dramatically.

Monthly Bankruptcies in Germany went from a low of 23 per month in 1923 to a high of 1,003 per month in 1926 (Babson 1941, p. 157).

It is not my purpose here to document the history of social unrest that existed within Germany during the 1920-23 inflation nor for the decade that followed. My only concern is to communicate to you the impact of those events on the daily lives of the people. The associated changes in lifestyle were devastating to the common man of that time and similar impacts could occur to you in your lifetime should runaway inflation occur again. It is in light of that requirement, the communication of past life experiences, that the following description is represented here. It describes in the vernacular of everyday events the inflation and its consequences for the common man.

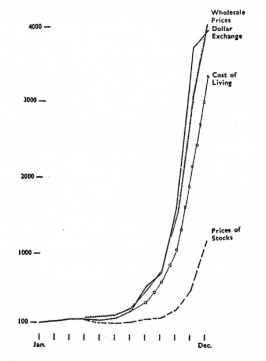

Fig. 1: January to December 1922, the height of the German inflation, showing how stocks went up but did not keep pace with the loss of value of the currency (Schultz 1972, p. 105).

Dr. Alexander Stein, now deceased, managed a hotel in Hungary during the 1920's hyperinflation. During that time they paid off the mortgage on their hotel with one month's receipts. After the Hungarian revolution in 1956, the communist government confiscated their hotel. Then it took three years for him and his wife to obtain exit visas. They immigrated to Canada with only their suitcases and at age 68 began a new life in a new country. He worked as the business manager of a large hotel in New Westminster, B.C., refusing to let his associates know his true age. He continued in that position until age 90 before retiring. He was a remarkable man.

The Florida Land Boom of 1926

The Florida Land Boom led to one of the great speculative crashes of the last century. Most people are not as aware of that crash as the stock market crash of 1929. Yet, the Florida land boom served as a preamble to the great crash to follow. Had the public heeded the lessons apparent in the land boom the crash of '29 might never have happened.

The reasons for the boom, lay in the seductive Florida climate, the rail line to the northeastern states, and the completion of the Dixie highway. In the early 1920's, increasing numbers of tourists began to trek to Florida. They were attracted by its carefree open life style, the proximity to the Caribbean Islands, where booze was legal, and its contrasts with the cold, slushy, smoky, urban corridor to the north. The attractions appealed not only to vacationers but to farmers and investors as well. The farmers perceived the potential for fruit and vegetable crops. The investors put their funds into developing vacation residences. Nineteen hundred and twenty four was the first year of the boom and by 1925 it was in full swing. The tourist invasion swelled to a migration with the number of visitors in 1925 perhaps as high as 10 million. The buying and selling of vacant lots became both a speculative fever and the way to instant wealth. This nirvana was possible because of the binder system. The binder was a form of purchase transfer which permitted the buyer to acquire the property with only a 10% down payment. Meanwhile the next payment was not due until the title had cleared. Since this procedure took up to six weeks, the buyer had that time free to locate a new buyer and sell his binder at a profit. The daily increase in prices was phenomenal, as much as 10% per day. This meant that a binder fee of $1,000 could purchase a $10,000 property which then sold a week later for $15,000 would yield a net return of $3,500 after broker fees. This $3,500 would represent a return of the original $1,000 capital plus a profit of $2,500 or 250% on the original investment. Meanwhile new subdivisions had lines of prospective buyers waiting for their chance to buy. By the time they could buy, they could sell their purchase for an immediate profit or conversely sell their place in line. Some properties increased in price by as much as 1,000 times before the crash came.

By 1926 the boom began to slacken. New buyers were not as common as previously, the slowing of demand was immediately reflected in increased difficulty of the selling of the binders. The end came with remarkable suddenness. Two hurricanes in October destroyed enormous amounts of property and further cast gloom on the long term potential for any development in South Florida. Most property owners went into default since the purchase prices agreed to greatly exceeded their ability to pay and there were no new buyers. By the time of the crash of 1929, 26 of Florida's cities were already in default.

As good an indicator as any of the nature of the crash is provided by the record of bank clearings for Miami:

1925	$1,066,528,000
1926	632,867,000
1927	260,039,000
1928	143,364,000
1929	142,316,000

(English and Cardiff 1979, p. 31)

All of the symptoms of a classic boom had been present. The buyers were speculators interested in a quick profit, rather than in developing the long term potential of the property. The speculators were operating on a high degree of margin which worked as long as new buyers kept arriving. The minute the flood of new buyers began tapering off the properties had no reason to maintain their value since that value was based on anticipated future increases in price rather than current income. The drop in the market between 1925 and 1928 approximated 50% per year. Since the late buyers were all in for a 10% down payment they lost everything and still the values plummeted.

My mother was teaching in a rural school in Kansas at the time land salesmen came to town promoting the values in Florida land by means of photos of prosperous farms. Out of her school of 30 families, 12 families sold their Kansas farms and bought Florida land sight unseen. Within a year 10 of those families had returned to Kansas, disillusioned and broke. Those investors who could see farther ahead pulled out only, in many cases, to lose their capital in the stock market crash three years later. The concept that the little man can get rich quickly, with minimal capital to begin with, is a concept that is typical of all booms. It is a concept that was proven false in the Florida Land Boom. The question is does the Florida experience bear any relevance to conditions today? We shall explore that question further a little later.

The Crash of '29—Hardly a Man is Now Alive

Everyone knows about the crash of '29. There is no need to review those happenings in detail since they are part of the folk history of America, or are they? In fact, hardly anyone is now alive who both experienced those times and is still influential in current affairs. In order to experience the crash as an adult one would have to have been at least 20 years of age in 1929 or past 90 today. Those with major responsibility for business affairs in 1929 would have been closer to 40 years of age, today no longer living. An exception is my Father-in-law, now 98, who has an excellent memory and has told me many times about the '29 crash and its aftereffects. Just to place all this in perspective, I was born in 1931. With my Father-in-law as an exception, those of us concerned today with the '29 crash have to rely on history for our knowledge and we all know that historical accounts are selective in what they record and emphasize as important.

However, in spite of this historical bias it is not my intent here to rechronicle those events. That has been done admirably by John Kenneth Galbraith(1955) and I recommend that you read his summary. Another excellent source is Federick Lewis Allen's Only Yesterday (1931). What I shall attempt to do here is to isolate those events which seem to have been typical of the crash and may serve as our guide in similar situations both today and into the future.

As we have seen, the late 1920's was a time of both widespread prosperity and widespread speculation. The era featured "peace and prosperity" and as the decade progressed the emphasis increasingly shifted from "prosperity" to the "accumulation of wealth" and "conspicuous consumption." It was an era which was typified by the concept that the average man could become rich. This attitude first appeared in the Florida Land Boom and then the focus of attention shifted to the stock market. A primary characteristic of that time was that speculation as a way to wealth seized the interests and imagination of the public. No longer were bellboys, plumbers, secretaries, and others content to do their jobs in exchange for an adequate living. They had glimpsed that dream of wealth and many succumbed to its charms. As the decade progressed and many profited quickly and handsomely, even the conservative financial institutions redefined their rules and goals to get a piece of the action. This then is our first observation and we shall ask later if a similar speculative fever exists today.

A second pattern of the times was the action of the market-place. The stock market recovered from a recession in 1921-22 by mounting slow and steady gains until 1925. After that date the increase in the market averages climbed more steeply and thus daily price action yielded faster and faster profits to the traders. After 1927 the market began to be more volatile. Rapid price increases were often matched by sharp corrective downturns, although the overall trend was still higher (Fig. 2,3). A similar trend had also been characteristic of the Florida Land Boom. These trends are directly associated with the influx of speculation.

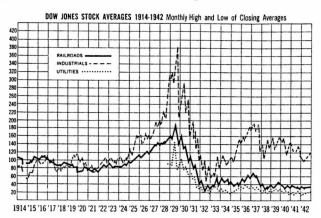

Fig. 2 (Patterson 1965, p. 2)

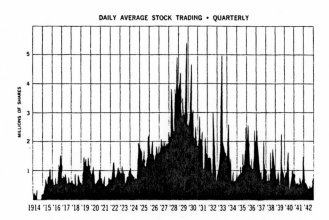

Fig. 3 Volume in stock trading. Note how the increase in volume is closely correlated with the increase in price and availability of credit between 1924 and 1929 (Patterson 1965, p. 3)

Fueling the speculative boom was the initiation of new techniques to permit speculators to function more freely. The first of these was the brokers loan. Funds were obtained from banks by brokers. These funds were used to purchase stocks and the stocks were then pledged as collateral for the loans. The stock buyers (speculators) typically put up 50% of the purchase price and borrowed the rest by means of the brokers loans. Everyone benefited, as long as prices went up. The banks borrowed their funds from the Federal Reserve at 5% and loaned them out at rates that normally ranged between 6% and 12%. At one point in 1928 the interest rate on these "call" loans peaked at 20%. The speculator could easily afford these rates since doubling in the price of his stock netted him a 200% return on his invested capital prior to payment of commissions. The brokers rejoiced as well since the loans were securely backed by the securities held and they were collecting a commission on all transactions. The margin requirement of 50% meant that everyone could buy twice as much stock which doubled the volume of business and caused prices to increase even more. Late in the boom there were too many buyers and not enough stocks to go round. The net result of the brokers loans was to permit the common man to "get in on the action." This was identical in effect to the binder system in the Florida Land Boom. Everyone could participate, even on a small scale, and therefore everyone had the chance to get rich. By 1929 the volume of broker loans totaled more than $7 billion, up from $1 billion in the early twenties, and $4 billion as late as June 1928 (Galbraith 1955, p. 26).

The hidden worm in the apple, of course, was the "call" provision. If the value of the stocks declined below the amount of the loan then the broker had the right to call for more funds from the stock owner to support the loan. If those funds were not forthcoming then the broker sold the stock in order to pay off the loan. During the '29 crash the calls for more margin led to large numbers of stock holders being sold out which depressed the market further, leading to more margin calls, more sales, lower prices, etc. As the market broke the margin calls became a self-feeding monster.

Meanwhile back to the problem of not enough stocks. This was solved by the formation of investment trusts. The trusts were new corporations set up to buy stocks. They sold stock to the public, often at inflated prices, and then used the proceeds to buy stocks and bonds. These trusts were frequently leveraged to permit their stock to increase geometrically as the value of their holdings increased. The trusts solved the limited stock supply problem. They were highly successful as stocks went up, therefore they increased rapidly in number. At the beginning of 1927 there were 160 trusts doing business, by 1928 there were 300, by 1929 the number had expanded to 486 and new trusts were being organized at the rate of one per day (Galbraith 1955, pp. 53-55). The action of the trusts pumped enormous amounts of new money into the market which eventually totaled $11 billion by the fall of 1929, an eleven fold increase in trust holdings since the beginning of 1927 (Galbraith 1955, p.55). The trusts were self eviscerated during the crash as a result of their own organizational structure. The leverage that permitted the trusts' own stocks to gain geometrically in value as their holdings increased in value lost value in equal manner. Long before the holdings of the trusts were worthless the stocks of the trusts themselves had lost all value. The leverage worked as rapidly in reverse as it had worked previously in its precipitous climb.

During the climb there was little governmental alarm or caution taken to prevent speculation. We have cited how the banks profited on the brokers loans. The Federal Reserve expressed concern but failed to take positive action. Even a slight increase in the rediscount rate (the rate banks pay the Federal Reserve for funds they borrow) would have had a deflationary effect. However the counterargument that such action would have a restrictive and thus negative effect on legitimate business prevailed. Only late in the summer of 1929 was the rediscount rate increased from 5% to 6%, action which was both too little and too late. In addition the Federal Reserve Board took a narrow definition of its role. Its "job" was not to curb speculation but only to regulate the availability of credit in the daily conduct of business. Further the Fed did not exercise any control over corporate funds that were loaned to brokers for speculative purposes. Eventually those corporate funds actually exceeded the amount of broker loans obtained from banks. The net position of the Fed was that while they deplored the widespread speculation, they believed that it would be a self-correcting phenomenon which did not endanger the long-term financial health of the nation. Later events proved their view to have been myopic indeed!

Another major aspect of the period both before and after the crash was the role of economic authorities and representatives of the government. The list was topped by President Coolidge. In his message to Congress December 4, 1928 he stated, "In the domestic field there is tranquility and contentment . . . and the highest record of years of prosperity" (Galbraith 1955, p. 6). He was followed by Professor Irving Fisher, Joseph Lawrence, Charles E. Mitchell, and many others as well as the Harvard Economic Society; all of whom predicted not only prosperity but stated that stock values were fundamentally sound. Even after the crash came, the predictions were for a quick "recovery," "a return to normalcy," "the end of the downturn is in sight," "the worst is over " "prosperity is just around the corner." Yet in the face of these optimistic pronouncements the market continued its downward slide for three years. What is relevant for our inquiry is the fact that these were all recognized authorities with influential positions and roles, yet they were wrong and their attempts to deal with reality failed miserably. Their eventual discreditation became a symptom of the times, all authority, banks, brokers, government, and economists alike fell into disrepute. This fact may be one reason why the ensuing depression went on so long before the turnaround came. Meanwhile other authorities such as Roger Babson who predicted during the boom the true course of events to come were instantly discredited because their views were contrary to those of the majority. Both of these phenomena bear attention in our current state of affairs. Those who predict difficult times ahead are hushed up or ignored while the establishment lets "the good times roll."

As Galbraith says (1955, p. 201), "But now, as throughout history, financial capacity and political perspicacity are inversely correlated. Long-run salvation by men of business has never been highly regarded if it means disturbance in the present. So inaction will be advocated in the present even though it means deep trouble in the future. Here, at least equally with communism, lies the threat to capitalism. It is what causes men who know that things are going quite wrong to say that things are fundamentally sound."

When the crash came it was presaged by several major phenomena. The daily volume in stock transactions increased dramatically. Further price swings became frequent. There were good days and bad days. The market always went back up but the trend of unrestrained price rises had been broken.

September 3, 1929, is the day assigned by history as the day the bull market of the 1920's came to an end. Its demise was quiet and relatively unnoticed. The first major price break occurred September 4 and was the result of a prediction of a crash by Roger Babson speaking to his Annual National Business Conference (Galbraith 1955, p. 91). The market rallied the following few days and sagged again on September 9. The weakness was attributed to technical readjustment. Throughout September and into October there was an ebb and flow of confidence. Post mortems of the crash attribute more or less effect to the statement of specific individuals or to specific events. The most relevant factors may be that industrial and factory production had peaked in June and home building which had been in a slump, declined further. The point has been made that these factors indicated that the economy was already into a depression prior to the crash. By late October the market volume was up but prices were weak. The large volume of transactions led to a late reporting of sales. With the ticker running late speculators couldn't even follow the declines in their paper holdings. Black Thursday, October 24, was the first day of panic with over 12 million shares changing hands. It was followed by an organized attempt by the central bankers to buy in and stabilize the market. Their efforts were successful and prices were steady through Friday and Saturday. Monday, October 28 began the next major sell off. By then the situation was out of control, with the margin calls triggering more margin calls spelling disaster. This disaster was followed by the worst day in the history of the stock exchange, Tuesday, October 29. The crash had come and history would never be the same, seemingly the good times were gone forever.

Two points are important to stress concerning the nature of the crash itself. The first is that the actual precipitating event or events that led to the first big sell off were in themselves irrelevant. The precipitating factor leading to the crash was excessive speculation. The actual day of reckoning was not dependent upon any specific events but more properly should be viewed as the result of chance. In this view if one precipitating cause hadn't appeared another would have done the job. Our second observation is that the sequence of events was not apparent to those involved. Only with the perspective of history is it possible to pinpoint the critical turning points. In summary the crash was not an event, it was a process which continued over a period of time, gradually worse, gradually more apparent, until panic set in followed by involuntary collapse. What we must remember is that between September 5, when Roger Babson's accurate prediction of the crash was soundly criticized in the national financial press, and Black Tuesday, October 24, there were only 44 days in which speculators could have taken preventative action.

The causes of the great boom and ensuing crash in 1929 have received considerable attention from subsequent economic scholars. The reasons cited include easy credit, over production by industry, war reparations, monetary policy, etc. Two items seem not to have been contributing causes. The first was inflation caused by deficit governmental spending. In fact between 1919 and 1930 the federal debt was reduced from $25 billion to $17 billion (Patterson 1965, p. 223). A second item not a contributory cause was commodity prices which actually were lower at the end of the decade than when the 20's began. However no analysis can ignore the crowd psychology that led to the speculative frenzy. It was this attitude that led perfectly sane individuals to believe that an era of prosperity had arrived in which businessmen no longer need fear recessions and the average individual had every reason to expect that he could become wealthy. One student of the boom states: "It seems that no matter how irrational a widely held belief may appear in retrospect only a mind of remarkable independence can resist its compelling force when it is flourishing. The general confidence in ever-rising stock prices with its supporting rationalization that justified speculation, was symptomatic of the phenomenon that Bernard Baruch and others have referred to as "the madness of crowds." Although still largely unexplained by behavioral scientists, this so-called "madness" must be taken into account in any attempt to explain major booms and panics" (Patterson 1965, pp. 224-5).

On the other hand if we refer to a strict economic appraisal of the cause and effect relationship we can do no better than to quote Carl Snyder. "Never a depression without a preceding boom. Never a boom and high prosperity without an outbreak of speculation. Never such an outbreak that has not ended in a financial crisis. Check the speculation in time, and we shall have no serious depressions" (Patterson 1965, p. 243).

These observations lead us to summarize as follows: The events leading up to a crash are of long duration. The crash is the result of the cumulative effects of financial factors and speculative actions carried out over a long period of time. This period of time is so long that changes in credit, interest rates, buying and selling procedures which have become increasingly speculative, are viewed as perfectly reasonable and normal. These speculative tendencies are then carried far beyond the capacity of the economy to absorb them without dislocation. Owing to the speculative excesses there can be no readjustment to normalcy since what had become normal is an imbalance. When the crash does come it comes with a swiftness startling to behold. It has already occurred before a downtrend can be identified. After the euphoria we can perceive the Economic Cycle has reasserted itself (Fig. 4).

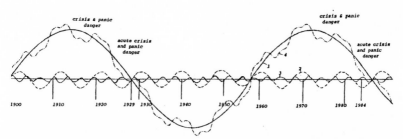

Fig. 4 The 20th Century Business Cycle and Crisis Points (Calculated Path) (Schultz 1972)

The Dot Com Bubble

You've just read about the bubbles in the past, the French Connection, the Runaway Inflation of 1923, the Florida Land Boom, and the Crash of '29. The Dot Com Bubble is different. The reason that it is different is that you have lived through it (Mandell 2000). Hardly a man is now alive who lived through the prior speculative bubble, that of 1929. My father-in-law is an exception. Now 98 years old, he vividly remembers how it was when people took their rent money to buy more stocks on margin. His memories of the boom and the subsequent depression have greatly influenced the opinions expressed in this book.

What is significant is that the same old rubrics reappeared in the 1990's. "Times are different," "The economic cycle has been repealed." "We're in a new era, the Information Age," "The old standards of value no longer apply," "So what that X Corporation doesn't show a profit, we'll make it up in volume." Given those attitudes, what Allen Greenspan, the Chairman of the Federal Reserve Bank, termed "Irrational Exuberance," anything was possible; "the sky's the limit"! The result was that the stock of companies operating at a loss was selling for 200 times or even 400 times *future projected* earnings.

The tragedy, of course, as it always is, is that these myths were believed by the average American. The stock market pundits said, "Buy, buy, the market has gone up 10% every year". And most of us believed them. All you had to do was put your 401K investments into high tech stocks, and presto-zappo, in ten years you could retire and move to that island paradise. Unfortunately, somewhere, along the way to the forum, as Zero Mostel pointed out, something happened. In this case, with the high price of tech stocks only held up by hot air, their price began to slide in the year 2000. Personally, I had long thought the market was too high and felt that a major correction was long overdue. The crash of 1987 was an example of a long expected correction that fit all the hallmarks of the beginning of a depression. The market sold off dramatically, a true crash. Then stocks began a slow downward slide which exactly matched that of the post 1929 slide; until March of 1988, at that point the Federal Reserve stepped in, liberalized credit and reversed the trend. However, all they actually accomplished was to fuel the inflationary fires and to postpone the inevitable depression. The reasons for the depression are simple; the overheated economy can only expand for so long. Eventually reality overtakes all of the overly optimistic forecasts. Looking backward, it seems to us totally ridiculous that during the Tulepmania, in the 1600's, ordinary Dutchmen exchanged everything they owned for a single rare tulip bulb which, when the crash came, became totally worthless. Yet, many 20th century Americans placed their faith on their economic future in High Tech stocks. Stocks were bought for their 401K plans at $60 to $80 per share, which after the crash of 2001-2 were selling for less than 60 cents.

Evidence of the extent of the 2000—2002 crash is presented dramatically in the graphs below (Fig. 5).

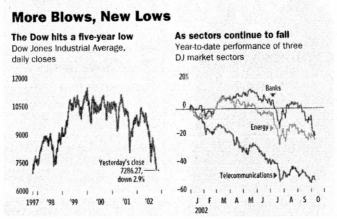

Fig. 5 The Stock Market decline 2000-2002, Wall Street Journal, *Oct. 10, 2002*

The lessons to be learned are several:

1. The economic cycle has not been repealed. Periods of boom times are always followed by crashes and recessions. The reason is that booms create a fever of speculation. Schemes that have no foundation in reality become, for a brief time, believable.

2. The belief that the masses can become wealthy is not realistic. At no time in human history has the general population accumulated wealth. True wealth is only accumulated by the few. In the book, "The Millionaire Next Door", it is revealed that only about 3% of the population, even in the 1990's, possessed true wealth. The Dot Com crash only punctuated that fact.

3. The third lesson is perhaps the most important: During the good times you must prepare for the bad times because they are surely coming.

4. During the good times the speculative excesses become so flagrant that later, after the return to reality, we look back

and ask ourselves, "how could we have been so stupid as to believe in those sky high evaluations?" Examples include Enron, World Com, and other High Tech companies that went belly up.

5.   The predominant emotion during a speculative boom is greed. Greed causes corporate executives to engage in fraud, which is bad enough. However the greed in the average investor causes them to overlook the corporate greed, at least, until after the crash. So we are all guilty.

6.   The next phase of the economic cycle, after the boom, is a crash, followed by a depression. We will examine the latter next.

CHAPTER 3
THE DEPRESSION OF THE
1930's

Causes

Having reviewed the crash of 1929 we have not yet explained or identified the causes of the ensuing depression. Economists since that time have sought to identify why the depression of the '30's was so severe and lasted so long, in contrast to earlier monetary and speculative collapses. At the time it was the perception of those with expertise that the economy was ready to recover, that "prosperity was just around the corner", yet the bad times persisted. In a study of the monetary factors, Temin (1976, p. 169) states that monetary factors were not responsible. Interest rates declined from 6% to 2% between the crash of 1929 and the fall of 1931. Further the money supply fell in 1930 and 1931 as well. Even so the decline of prices was greater than the decline in the money supply. Therefore there was an increase in buying power. While the crash did not specifically cause the depression it reduced individual wealth and hence purchase of consumable items. A further contributing factor was reduction in business borrowing; inventories were reduced, production was reduced, and construction of new facilities was postponed. However, these can just as properly be viewed as results as causes.

Agriculture was also a contributor since agricultural income was down and had been low throughout the '20's.

According to Patterson (1965, pp. 21-22) the decline in consumer spending was more significant as a cause of the depression than any specifically monetary factors.

Charles P. Kindleberger (1973, p. 291) has posed the question as follows:

> [W]hat produced the world depression of 1929, why was it so widespread, so deep, so long? [W]as the 1929 depression the consequence of United States monetary policy or a series of historical accidents?

His explanation is that the depression was so wide, so deep and so long because the international economic system was unstable.

> The world economic system was unstable unless some country stabilized it, as Britain had done in the nineteenth century and up to 1913. In 1929, the British couldn't and the United States wouldn't. When every country turned to protect its national private interest, the world public interest went down the drain, and with it the private interests of all. (Kindleberger 1973, pp. 291-292)

My own explanation is more intuitive and psychologically oriented. What I perceive happened is that the 1929 crash so damaged the credit system that everyone went into a state of shock. In effect people lost faith in credit as a means to conduct business. There was a reversion to a cash economy and there wasn't enough cash to go around. It became a self-feeding syndrome in which insufficient cash led to insufficient demand. The reduction in demand led to reduction in sales. With reduction in sales inventories did not need to be replenished. Therefore workers were laid off. The more workers out of work the fewer buyers, so the deflationary spiral continued. This explanation may be termed a crisis in confidence. It was psychologically based and it paralyzed the economy of the world for an entire decade. It could happen again.

The Nature of the Depression

The Depression was a time of great personal crises, deprivation, and suffering. Millions of people were out of work and the government seemed helpless to do anything. Between 1929 and the election of Franklin Roosevelt in 1932 the economy plunged to the depths. The Hoover approach was the trickle down theory—support the financial institutions and big industry and the rest of the economy would recover and fare well. It didn't happen and amidst periodic predictions that the worst was over millions more joined the soup kitchen lines, wore out their shoes looking for work, moved across the country hitching rides on freight trains, and ended up in hobo jungles. There are several good references on the privation of the Depression and I will not attempt to add to those (Broadfoot 1971, Goldston 1968, etc). My purpose here is to attempt to summarize the nature of the Depression. People have since that time blocked out the memories of those difficult times and those born since 1940 know little about the hardships that were endured. In fact today's affluent society cannot even imagine what it was like and it is my purpose here to inform them by means of the following brief description.

My personal memories of the Depression are minimal. I remember my mother stating that their five dairy cows, purchased for $150 went for $15 each three years later when their dairy business failed. My grandfather lost everything and he had been a large landowner engaged in farming. He started anew by pushing a cart around town full of tools with which he did plumbing. In another situation, my mother and father were sitting on the porch steps discussing what they would do after the bank repossessed their combine. Just then the mailman delivered my father's World War I bonus from the State of Illinois; more than enough to pay the next installment on the combine! However it wasn't enough in the long run and they eventually lost it and went out of farming altogether.

In 1934, I was three years old. My parents were running the dairy and didn't have any money. Even so they decided to take a well-earned week's vacation. They loaded up the model A with canned food and enough cans of motor oil and headed for Colorado Springs, 400 miles away. We stayed in a tourist court at Manitou where the cabins rented for 25 cents per night. My father only had $3 when they left home, yet somehow we made it. I can remember seeing Seven Falls, the Garden of the Gods, the running stream, the bear in the stone cage, and eating breakfast flakes at the picnic table. We didn't visit the Cave of the Winds since there was an admission charge.

After failing in the farming-dairy business, my parents operated filling station-corner grocery stores from 1935 to 1940. About 1940 I can remember my job was to fill the gasoline pumps by pumping the handle on the side of the pump. This is the same kind of pump they now have on display in the Smithsonian. I well remember the day a truck with a long pipe sticking out of the bed broke the glass container in all three of our pumps. We lost 30 gallons of gas plus the glass containers, a crushing loss! You can still see the remnants of those gas stations across the country. There was one at every road corner at intervals of a few miles. Thousands were trying to eke out a living selling gas and groceries. I remember when the Depression ended—for us; it was about 1941 or even 1942. My dad started buying factory made cigarettes and stopped rolling his own with Bull Durham.

In order to supplement my memory of the depression the following descriptive accounts are presented. I believe only by reading the actual statements of those who suffered through the depression will you be able to comprehend its deprivations and hardships. In fact my parents, and I suspect most parents did the same, never told me many details of the privations they suffered. Their experiences were simply too degrading to bear repeating; as you read the following selected samples of fairly typical quotes from a cross section of the population of the 1930's, I'm sure you will understand what I mean.

"Hoover stated: 'Many persons left their jobs for the more profitable one of selling apples.'" (Golston 1967 p.49)

"In 1929, 3.2% of the labor force was unemployed."(Chandler 1970, p. 5)

"By the spring of 1930—six months after the crash—over 4 million Americans were out of work." (Goldston 1967, p. 47)

"Between 1930 and 1932 over 5,000 banks failed, 21.5% of the U.S. total number of banks." (Chandler 1970, p. 83)

"U.S. imports dropped by 63% by 1933." (Chandler 1970, p. 101)

"By the summer of 1932, when stock prices reached their trough, they were 83% below their peak in September 1929 and 72% below the lowest levels reached in November 1929." (Chandler 1970, p. 23)

"By December, 1931, unemployment reached 13.5 million—almost one third of the American work force."(Goldston, p. 50)

"New construction dropped by 80.2%." (Chandler 1970, p. 25)

"Unemployment rates for blacks reached a high of 75% in some cities."(Chandler 1970, p. 40-41)

"By mid 1930 the depression was world wide and by 1932 at least 30 million people were unemployed."(Chandler 1970, p.11)

"Dairy farmers dumped milk rather than sell it for 2 cents a quart." (Goldston 1968, p. 66)

"Let me assert my firm belief that the only thing we have to fear is fear itself—nameless, unreasoning, unjustified terror which paralyzes needed efforts to convert retreat into advance. This nation asks us for action now..." Franklin Roosevelt, March 4, 1933. (Goldston 1968, p. 89)

These statements document some of the major facts of the depression, millions out of work, unable to meet their mortgage payments, and unable to find enough to eat. The industrial production was idling at half speed and those still employed making do on half salaries. Meanwhile the efforts of the Hoover administration were ineffective, largely because the true seriousness of the situation was never fully comprehended, as the following quote demonstrates:

"What the country needs is a good, big laugh. There seems to be a condition of hysteria. If someone could get off a good joke every ten days I think our troubles would be over"—Herbert Hoover. (Goldston 1968, p. 47)

The Roosevelt administration brought in monetary reform, public works programs, and relief payments. Even so the recovery was slow and the nation never really came out of the Depression until the beginning of World War II when everyone went back to work producing military supplies.

Meanwhile, throughout the 1930's the human suffering went on as documented in the next series, "The Social Burden", of selected personal remembrances and contemporary statements.

The Social Burden

"Seventeen thousand New York families were being evicted per month in 1932."(Bendiner 1967, p. 16)

"One of my jobs was to walk over after dark to the garden of the family that looked after the nearest grain elevator, a mile away, and steal carrots, radishes, anything that was growing. I never got caught because their dog was friendly. Never have a friendly dog in a depression." (Broadfoot 1973, p. 7)

"I remember not going to school my fifth grade, about 12 years old, because I didn't have shoes. My sister Helen went though, because she could use the ones I grew out of." (Broadfoot 1973, p. 79)

"The director called a meeting about this strike business and the superintendent told them, 'Let 'em all quit. I can replace 'em all by tomorrow morning if they do.' We all grumbled a lot, but what could we do? We stayed on the job and kept getting 14 cents an hour. That was the Depression for you." (Broadfoot 1973, p. 2)

"Six million Shirley Temple dolls were sold at $3 to $30 each." (Time Life 1969, p. 94)

"Oh yes, these dolls. I'd stand and watch the faces of those little girls, from about four or five right up to about eleven. Some used to come at opening time and just stand there looking at those pink-cheeked, golden-haired lovely Shirley Temples. Little faces, they needed food. You could see a lot who needed a pint of milk a day a thousand times more than they needed a Shirley doll. They'd stare for hours. We tried to shush them away but it didn't do any good. They'd go once around Toyland and be back. This mind you, went on day after day, until some of the girls thought they would go crazy. One girl had a crying fit just over that, those hundreds of poor kids who would never own a Shirley Temple in a hundred years. They were lucky if they had breakfast that morning, or soup and bread that night."(Broadfoot 1973, p. 265)

This may be a familiar quote:

"The decay spreads over the state, and the sweet smell is a great sorrow on the land....and in the eyes of the hungry there is a growing wrath. In the souls of the people the grapes of wrath are filling and growing heavy, growing heavy for the vintage." John Steinbeck (Goldston 1968, p. 152)

One Man's Experiences

Researchers studying the depression note the lack of written coverage of those times. There seems to have been a general attitude that once the Depression ended, it should be forgotten as quickly as possible. Others, and Sewall Avery, the former head of Montgomery Ward, is an outstanding example, were so traumatized by the Depression that they were never able to adjust to the prosperity that came after 1941. Those individuals kept all their assets in cash and could not revert to a credit economy. While we have quantities of statements about the Depression by the press and by the politicians, the average man in the street wasn't saying much or at least recording his opinions for prosperity. One man, W.A. Davis, was an exception to this general rule. He kept a diary, beginning in 1928 and continuing throughout the Depression and World War II, with fairly consistent entries until 1950. His Depression experiences began in Ohio, continued in Las Vegas, Nevada, where he worked as a freelance photographer during the building of Boulder Dam. He moved on to Los Angeles and a relief job as a W.P.A photographer. He tried his hand at gold mining and stump ranching in the woods in Oregon. All those efforts ended in failure and he returned to the family farm in Ohio until World War II brought factory employment as a machinist and tool and die maker. Only a few selected samples of statements from his diary are reproduced below, but they illustrate his enduring industriousness in his attempts to work for a living. My purpose in using excerpts from his diary is not to chronicle his life, nor to duplicate experiences detailed in previous sections. My purpose is to document the futility of it all in the 1930's—the average man's inability to cope with the difficulties of the times, no matter what he put his hand to or how hard he tried.

> 1929: I was digging ditches for the gas company in Ohio at $8 a day and wearing a $10 silk shirt while doing it. I thought the good times would never end.

> March 4, 1933: This day at 10 a.m. marked the inauguration of Franklin D. Roosevelt as President of the United States. Never before in the history of our country has a man undertook this office when conditions throughout the country were at such a low ebb as they are today. Our national budget is far from being balanced and we are at the present time plunging at the rate of over $200,000 an hour into debt. Prohibition has been repealed subject to ratification of two thirds of the states. Eighteen million people today are in the ranks of the unemployed out of our 130 million people. Nearly every state in the union

has a moratorium on farm and city home mortgage foreclosure. Nearly every bank in the U.S. is under a holiday or restricted withdrawals which are limited to 5%. Many cities are using script and California is making this preparation. Labor disputes and strikes flare up throughout the land. Prices of all farm produce are the lowest which has been recorded since 1897. Technocracy has sprung up with a plan to reconstruct the government. Japan is at present fighting for a piece of China and several other nations are eyeing one another up. Debts from the European nations are still owed to us and from out of all this haze this man promises to lead us out.

Sept. 19, 1934: Spent my last dime today and not having anything in the house to eat I applied for relief.

Sept. 26, 1934: Today I spent picking walnuts, picked three bags which they paid me 40 cents a sack or $1.20. Farmer gets 7.5 cents a pound for them. Our neighbor loaned us a stove.

Nov. 29, 1934: Have been panning a little gold at Newhall and Saugus.

Jan 27, 1935: Still on relief getting $5.40 a week for groceries.

Mar. 4, 1935: Delano and I have been panning gold up at Saugus and here's our return

1st day—15 cents

2nd day—32 cents

3rd day—45 cents

4th day—75 cents

Mar. 25th, 1936: I started working on the 20th on W.P.A. project as a photographer. Division of Visual Education

Dec. 15, 1936: Expect to be laid off Jan 11th, 1937, from the W.P.A.

Mar. 26, 1937: Received word yesterday that I failed to pass the 75 grade mark in Civil Service. Grade was 54.99. Advertised my place for sale and figured on taking a trip this summer.

Sept. 2, 1938: The wife and I have just put in 6 days hop picking and our earnings were $9.52 as they paid one and a quarter cents per pound. Some wages. Most every day its over 90 degrees by noon and we are trying to sell our place here and go back east this fall.

The Depression—An Appraisal

The Depression began without warning, as a three-year long slump in everything, prices, wages, demand, supply, inventories, incomes and expectations. Amid predictions that the worst was over, the worst got even worse. Those involved had no idea how bad it could get and before it was over more than a decade had elapsed and millions had lost everything they owned. Students since then have attempted to identify the cause of the Depression with limited success. Furthermore there is lingering doubt that the New Deal was adequate to reverse the economic tide. Only the beginning of World War II provided what was needed, universal employment. Finally there is no guarantee that a similar situation could not occur again. All that is required for a future major depression to begin is a major crisis of public confidence in our credit system, our currency, our balance of payments, our mode of public expenditures, or doubt that the government can pay its debts.

PART III

How It Is

Today

In this section we will review the basic economic factors in operation today. We will focus on the current major problems, employment, inflation, interest rates, the energy shortage, the tax revolt, others. Prior to that, however, we must examine the basic economic cornerstones of our financial system in order that we may understand the limitations our government faces in its attempts to deal with the problems.

A final chapter in this "How It Is" section reports on those elements in our society which, in one way or another, are contributing to the problems. Our purpose in such an extended review of how things are today is to determine how bad things really are today, and, through comparison with our prior historical examples, to estimate how bad things will get in the future.

CHAPTER 4
HOW OUR ECONOMY
WORKS

The Great Juggling Act, or Godzilla Meets the Economic Indicators

Passage of the Full Employment Act of 1946 has led our government into a dilemma from out of which they cannot extricate themselves, nor us, nor can they see the way out, even though they think they can, or pretend they can, or have fooled themselves into believing they can. I could write that sentence with greater clarity but its fumbling confused style best describes the great Federal Juggling Act. No Moses could lead our government into the Promised Land since that promise entails simultaneously—full employment and control over inflation.

A final aspect of the credit equation is consumer credit. This is the buying ability conferred on the individual simply by his filling out a credit reference form. Once it is filled out the firm grants you a credit card or loan with no questions asked. You have approval to instantly spend from $1,000 to $10,000 or so at Sears, Wards, Penny's, your favorite gas station or restaurant or any business that accepts Visa, Bankamericard, American Express, etc. Added to the credit cards are the installment purchases of appliances and automobiles. Put it all together and the totality of consumer credit burdens almost every family in the land. Recent studies indicate that 23% of personal income is committed to installment debt, a total of more than one trillion dollars.

Two aspects of this mountain of debt are troublesome: 1) we are getting deeper and deeper into debt, and 2) the deeper we are in debt the less disposable income we have available to acquire new consumer items. This lack of buying power threatens the entire economy since manufacturing and retail sales firms cannot prosper if they have no one to sell to.

One estimate reports that installment debt accounts for 69% of current disposable income, that's the part left after taxes and other deductions. This means that we have very little residual buying power left. Meanwhile, and this is the crucial problem, inflation in the cost of necessities like food, clothing, gasoline, and housing is continuing.

The only place left in the family budget to squeeze out the extra cost of necessities lies in that 31% of disposable income that is not already committed to installment debt. The future looks bleak for sales of consumer items since a higher percentage of personal income will have to be paid out for the inflation increased costs of necessities. This also means there will be less and less borrowing to buy consumer items just to keep up with your neighbors. Further, it means there will be less disposable income left over to get out of debt. It is a double bind, bad for the economy and bad for the individual consumer.

Here is the problem stated in stark simplicity that even tiny children can understand. As unemployment decreases, consumer prices increase. As unemployment increases, consumer prices decrease (Fig. 6). The Full Employment Act, therefore, in its simplest meaning, means a commitment of our government to a continuation of inflation. However, quote, our government is also committed to "fighting inflation." The economic indicators, as represented by the GNP, unemployment rate, rate of inflation, interest rates, money supply, etc., clearly record that you can't have it both ways at the same time.

You cannot simultaneously reduce unemployment and inflation.

Fig.6: *Inflation and Unemployment Changes, 1950 to 1975(CED 1976, p. 13). As Unemployment increases consumer prices decrease, and vice versa.*

This leads our, quote, "leaders" into the great juggling act wherein they try to "fine tune" the economy by changing the money supply or interest rates or by selling gold or some other device to strengthen the dollar in an attempt to keep both of these incompatible elements under a semblance of control. Godzilla, of course, is the ultimate reality which is expressed so well in the graph above. Godzilla rears his ugly head every time there has been any success toward meeting one of the goals, either reduction of unemployment or inflation, since for every economic action there is an opposite and equal reaction. In this case both of these elements, unemployment and inflation are politically *unacceptable.* This means that in their fine tuning the monetary policy boys and the administration must simultaneously complain that the rate of inflation is unacceptably high while increasing the money supply like mad in order to reduce unemployment. They know that the pumping up of the money supply will lead to even higher inflation in the future but maybe they can pass on that unwelcome political legacy to the next administration. Another gambit they employ is to focus on only one of these twin problems at a time and pretend that they are unrelated. They thus issue only statements as to what actions they are taking to "reduce unemployment," or "reduce inflation," but say nothing about the long term results of their actions on the other factor.

The solution of course is to abandon these attempts to control both factors simultaneously. Another way to state this is that passage of the Full Employment Act guarantees continuing inflation. In order to control inflation we must abandon the effort to control the level of employment. Only with the supply and demand equation left free to work in the marketplace can we expect to bring inflation under control. In short, only with unemployment levels left free to rise, can we expect some good news on the fight against inflation. Even here the system may have been out of balance for so long that equilibrium cannot easily be established. John Kenneth Galbraith (Galbraith and Salinger 1978, pp. 31-46) questioned whether the market, in a true economic sense continues to function. He cites the oligopolic control of prices by large corporations coupled with inflationary expectations as factors preventing the establishment of prices in the market according to the laws of supply and demand. The result of such control mean that prices go up no matter what happens since the large corporations *control* the market.

John D. Harper has perhaps stated the problem in this most succinct form (CED 1976, p. 84):

> The most significant change has been increased government intervention in the domestic economic system in an effort to force the private sector to perform in some theoretical noninflationary manner while the public sector continues on its inflationary binge.

His statement refers to the politically inspired financial actions of the Johnson, Nixon, Ford and later administrations and their results.

Jack Anderson, in a column in the Washington Post, cites the Carter administration's efforts on the inflation front as an "Economic Kindergarten".

Anderson's summary is:

> The Carter theory is that over spending by consumers causes inflation, and the only solution is simultaneously to keep wages down and make the price of such major items as fuel oil and credit so high fewer people will be able to afford them.

These analyses all have one thing in common, they stress the symptoms rather than the cure. This suggests that for whatever reasons fine-tuning is not the answer. We need a return to basic economic acts and relationships.

If we return to our graph, we perceive that there have been points of crossover. These are times when the unemployment and inflation rates were the same. Presumably these represent points at which the system was in balance. These points were:

Year	Inflation and Unemployment Rate
1952	3.2%
1967	3.8%
1971	5.2%
1972	5.5%
1975	8.0%

What is immediately apparent is that the points of equilibrium are not all the same. This suggests that some other factor is at work. The most obvious factor would seem to be the increase in the money supply, no matter what the reason, to fund federal deficits, buy imported oil, etc.

If we examine the correlation between the money supply and the consumer price index (Fig. 7), which is as good an indication of inflation as any, we perceive a close linkage.

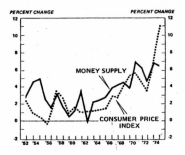

Fig. 7 Correlation between increases in the Money Supply and the Consumer Price Index. (Klein and Wolman 1975, p. 35)

Increases in the money supply are shortly thereafter, six to eighteen months, followed by a corresponding increase in the rate of inflation. Therefore, it seems possible, given the limitations in the market outlined by Galbraith, that equilibrium could be achieved at a lower level than at present if:

1.   The rate of unemployment was left to seek its own level, and

2.   The focus was placed in managing the money supply so that it could not increase at a precipitous rate. Various authorities place the annual increase in the money supply which is necessary for the growth in the GNP at 1% to 2%. All growth above that level is inflationary.

The political consequences of this type of action are considered "unacceptable", since presumably, the total number of people out of work would increase. Therefore, we can look forward to continued and fruitless "juggling" and "fine tuning" and in addition, the frequent appearances of Godzilla.

We can also ask whether or not the establishment of wage and price controls could be effective on the great juggling act. Klein and Wolman (1975, pp. 163-173) in an extensive study of the effects of wage and price controls are not optimistic. They state that in fact the political history of age and price controls to date feature two elements. The controls are only placed in effect when the economy is already trending downward. Therefore the political gambit is one of seeming to take a strong take-charge position on the part of the administration when in fact they are simply seeking to take credit for events which were already occurring. In addition the record is clear that wage and price controls are in fact inflationary since they cause prices to be raised prematurely in anticipation of the controls. Further, when controls are removed there is an explosive upward push to prices and wages as a result of pent up demand.

In summary, our review of the great juggling act leads us to conclude that it will continue but its success will be limited. We shall now look into what governmental spokesman are saying while they are in the midst of the juggling act. The question is how they attempt to justify what we have seen is an impossible task.

Conversations with Charlie

Back in March 1978, I was in the Sam Rayburn Congressional Office Building attending a government seminar hosted by our local congressman. The luncheon speaker was Charles Schultz, the Chairman of The President's Council of Economic Advisors, and he presented a scenario in which the monetary policy boys at Treasury and the Federal Reserve come on stronger than dirt and "whip inflation"; not now—which was Gerald Ford's mistake, predicting victory so soon that when it didn't happen he ended up with egg on his face—Charles Schultz's target date was 1982, which was still safely in the future. The game plan consisted of simultaneously stimulating the economy through a tax cut, plus a gradual reduction in the rate of unemployment resulting from administrative stimulation in the hiring process, such as tax credits. These curves converged at the rate of about 1% per year each, which brought us into balance about 1982 from a rate of inflation and unemployment of 6% each at that time. I spoke from the audience at this point and asked how reliable were his figures since the Wall Street Journal the day before had published an article which revised those figures (inflation and unemployment upward, and the growth of the GNP downward by about 1% each). In short, my question was if this whole plan depended on those figures, then they better be reliable. I was in my Clark Kent suit so Charlie didn't know that I was really your favorite financial reporter, Al Horatio; he thought I was just another car dealer from the sticks. His answer was that it was true, the figures had been revised but they were still good with an accuracy of plus or minus 2%. Since his whole plan was based on a 2% favorable change in the indicators per year, and his input data were subject to an error of equal magnitude, the plan was really little more than a fond hope. Since then his whole scenario has been roundly discredited with inflation reaching as high as 13%. My reason for telling this little story is to point out that if you can't believe the financial advice you get from the Chairman of the President's Council of Economic Advisors, than who can you trust?

By way of an answer I must again refer to statements by Charles Schultz. In an article in the Washington Post he supported the spring 1979 increase in the legal limit to the U.S. national debt. At that moment the U.S. government had reached its legal debt ceiling and therefore could not pay federal employees or pensioners.

Congress was debating the issue when Schultz came forth with his endorsement to increase the debt ceiling. His stated reason was that an increase in the debt ceiling would combat inflation! Now this kind of reasoning is analogous to fighting fire with gasoline! Additional deficit spending is the sure way to increase inflation. Therefore we must ask why Schultz made such a statement. The reason must be a political one since his statement makes no economic sense whatsoever. The reason for political statements is based on the concept of the self-fulfilling litany, the belief that utterance of the statement will have an influence on the course of future events. In short, the statement is not made to inform or explain, but is an attempt to change reality either by causing people to take action or, if that is not possible, at least to change their thinking on a specific issue. Even the introduction of confusion into the situation may serve a political end. What Schultz did was add confusion as to the true causes of inflation so then he could launder the dirty skirts of the federal administration.

This course of action further includes the concept of "fine tuning." This idea is that the federal administration can control the march of economic events by small adjustments in interest rates, the money supply, taxes, etc. The overall concept is an attempt to control the economic cycle and indeed, eliminate it forever. Such a belief leads the administration into the ridiculous posture of contradicting its own actions and statements periodically. The administration hopes that by saying things are better than they really are that will change reality. The truth is the administration is not in control of the economy, they only think they are. That's what administrations have done in the past and the Bush administration is attempting today when they talk of the "recovery."

In conclusion, we must recognize that any economic statements released by the federal administration are designed not to report the facts but to alter the facts. Often such statements are no more than wishful thinking and are analogous to saying you aren't pregnant since it doesn't show yet.

White Hats or Black Hats? The Federal Reserve

The Federal Reserve Board is that unit of our government set up to control our credit system. The role of the Federal Reserve consists of regulating the amount of money in circulation which has the effect of stimulating or depressing business activity. These actions are now viewed as crucial in the stimulation or control of the rate of inflation. Largely as a result of writings by Milton Friedman and other monetarists, the money supply has come to be viewed as critical. Current views are that ideally the money supply should grow at the same rate as national production—about 2% per year. Such a target level provides sufficient capital to fund new business without an associated boom. Monetary growth below 2% leads to a recession while growth above that level is inflationary. Since 1970, the growth in the money supply has averaged close to 7% and has been as high as 18% (Fig. 8).

Crucial questions concern: 1) the ability of the Federal Reserve to control changes in the money supply, and 2) whether the Federal Reserve is in fact subject to political pressures to control the business climate to affect political ends.

Fig.8: Growth of the Money Supply (Anonymous)

The Fed can increase the money supply by lowering bank reserve requirements, by reducing the bank discount rate—the interest charged banks on funds they borrow, or it can buy securities—treasury bills, etc., on the open market. All of these techniques work to increase the money supply. What is unclear is the relationship between this "new money" and the economy in general. Meanwhile we continue to rely on the methods used by the Federal Reserve. Methods that attempt to regulate the supply and demand through increasing or decreasing interest rates. In time of galloping inflation, such methods seem to be both inadequate and to take too long to achieve the effects desired. In times of deflation they may also be too slow.

The traditional economic view is that interest rates are self regulating in the sense that they represent market "bid" for the use of money. As rates increase there is a decrease in demand which eventually brings the rates down again. This cycle fluctuates over time but it is based on the concept that the lender is paid for giving up, temporarily, the use of his funds. The borrower is willing to pay for this use since he can increase his facilities, his production, etc. and thereby afford to pay the cost of the borrowed funds out of his increased profits. That is standard economic theory. However, inflation has changed all that. No longer can the lender be assured of a return at x%, no longer does the borrower have to pay a fixed rent on borrowed funds, in times of high inflation he may even get to use those funds for free. What is even more amazing is that neither the lenders nor the borrowers know what their true interest return or costs will be when they agree on a legally binding loan! Inflation has placed both parties in the role of gamblers. If the rate of inflation equals or exceeds the interest rate then the borrower wins. If not then the lender received a true rent on his funds. However neither party knows in advance what the true rate of inflation will be, therefore both are casting their dice in the dark. If we subtract the rate of inflation from the interest rate then we can perceive what the true rate of return actually was. Most of the time since 1970 that return has fluctuated between 1% and 2% and briefly, in 1977, was even negative.

After inflation true interest rates have averaged between 1% and 4% since 1960. When we remember that these interest rates are taxable income, and that tax is levied on the entire interest paid, not just the true return after inflation, then we can perceive that much of the interest received since 1970 has in fact not represented a true return. In this inflationary scenario the winners are the borrowers since they are using the funds of others at minimal cost.

However, and this is even more important, since the borrowers, owing to inflation, pay little for the use of funds, we have lost the braking effect on borrowing that high interest rates have posed historically. The investment climate n the 1990's was highly speculative and the minimal cost of borrowing contributed immensely to that situation. At the same time the entire bond market is threatened since investors have not benefited by past performance. They need to know what the future rate of inflation will be so that they can compute their expected return. This is called the anticipated real rate. In recent years, as inflation has exceeded expectations, the real rate has been less than the anticipated real rate, therefore all bond holders have been losers.

Three major conclusions stem from this analysis. The first is that high interest rates, in the recent past were still not high enough to discourage excessive speculation. Second, the Federal Reserve has lost much of its control over inflationary events—unless it dramatically increases interest rates to a level which would decrease speculation. Given historic levels of real interest rates, that level would have to be in the vicinity of 4% real interest in order to dampen demand. Meanwhile, rampart speculation, especially in residential housing, continues. Our third conclusion is that when the nation's bankers, pension fund managers, bond investors, and bond underwriters are all *gambling* as to the true return on funds invested, our financial system is in serious danger. For example, when your payroll deductions are invested in a pension plan no one knows what the real increase in value, if any, will be in the future. Meanwhile, what influence, if any, does gold have on our financial system?

The Golden Escalator

Recently gold has been selling in the $300 plus price range. The low price for gold in 1978 was $132 an ounce. Financial articles have termed this price rise as both "speculative" and "baffling." I don't think either of those adjectives fits the situation. In my opinion the price rise in gold is both "predictable" and "logical." Why is this so, besides the fact that I've said it's so? The anti-gold forces proclaim such price action to be "madness," a "speculative boom" which has no basis in financial realities. They cite the fact that to profit in gold it must provide capital appreciation since it pays no interest or income and is, quote, "expensive to store, and insure". In my opinion the latter arguments are primarily a smoke screen put out by those who feel threatened by gold—they are promoting stocks or bonds and therefore gold poses an unattractive alternative, as they see it, since they aren't selling gold but something else. The people who trade in gold like Deak and Co., don't see it that way. They view gold as just another commodity which they buy and sell on a daily basis making a commission on both ends of the transaction. The difference of opinion then is in part is similar to that between the owners of two different games of chance at the local carnival. In fact gold costs little to store since it is very small relative to its value. Further a safe deposit box eliminates the need for insurance. If you buy bullion coins you also don't need any assay in order to sell it. So all of the objections are countered.

The questions we need to answer pertain to the long term potential for the price of gold and the function of gold in the international money market. These questions are intimately related and we shall try to explain how and why.

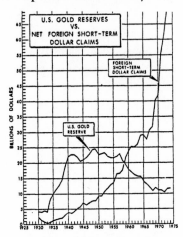

Fig. 9 U.S. Gold reserves vs. Net Foreign Short-Term Dollar Claims (Myers 1976, p. 63).

The pro-gold forces, called "gold-bugs" by their detractors, believe that gold has a legitimate role in international monetary control. It is their viewpoint that gold is the only commodity which has all of the attributes necessary for the real wealth which is necessary to provide support for a stable currency. Gold is and has always been viewed, since the invention of money, as the commodity which possesses the attributes best suited for money. It is beautiful, durable, easily divisible, and further it is rare and its supply cannot be easily increased. The last characteristic is what makes government uneasy about gold. Governments want to have total control over the ability to increase the money supply at will. Gold prevents this flexibility since it is costly to mine and the supply has always been very limited. Traditionally gold has either been used as a currency or as a fractional backing for the currency in circulation. This is the justification for the famous gold bars stored at Ft. Knox. Until 1971 the gold in Ft. Knox was used as a support for our currency(Fig. 9). Foreign governments could request payment in gold for dollars in their possession and our government would pay in gold. Since 1971 that privilege has been abolished by the U.S. government and by most other nations. South Africa is an exception since its gold Krugerand, which is still being minted, is an official issue of the government. Almost all transactions between governments today consist of the exchange of one form of printed paper(currency) for another form of printed paper. The rates of exchange established between any two currencies fluctuate on a daily basis as a result of differential production, crop failures, rates of inflation, etc. There are no stable currencies and this includes South Africa since the value of the Krugerand in terms of other currencies also fluctuates daily. These daily fluctuations create substantial problems for businesses since they must, in transacting international business, purchase supplies or accept payment for products sold in foreign currencies. Since these currencies do not have fixed value the business risks losing their profits from production in losses sustained in their currency exchange. A second problem concerns how to store your money received in a stable currency. If you have made a profit and wish to keep it for later use, in which currency should it be kept? In recent years Swiss francs, German marks, and Japanese yen have all been better repositories of wealth than the U.S. dollar. However, at present those countries have been hit with rising rates of inflation and their currencies have been losing value as a result.

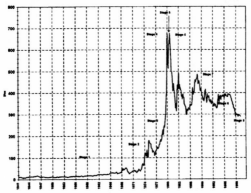

Fig. 10 Monthly Gold Index and Cash Gold: Nine Stages of the Long-Term Cycle From Bernstein (1999, Fig. 5.2).

Gold, because of its long term recognized value and scarcity, is the obvious alternative to use as a means of storing wealth. No other commodity or currency will serve as well. This fact means that gold has a permanent role to play in international monetary affairs. This is a long term role which, in the views of Donald Hoppe expressed earlier in this book, will eventually lead to an International Monetary Conference which will again agree to issue gold as backing for all major currencies. Viewed in this context then gold will continue to increase in value relative to paper currencies as long as:

1. There is no fixed relationship between gold and paper bills.

2. There is continuing inflation in the countries that issue paper currencies.

Since it is our opinion that inflation will be with us for the foreseeable future, we can assume that for that same interval the long term price trend of gold will be upward (Fig. 10). Meanwhile there are trends and countertrends in the gold price on a daily basis. For the short term gold goes down as well as up so it is possible to buy gold today at $300.00 per ounce and see it sell next month for $280.00. However the long-term trend is clearly upward. The important fact to remember is that there is no logical upward limit to the price of gold. It can go to $500.00 per ounce, $1,000.00, $100,000, $1 million, etc., There is no logical limit. What controls the eventual price of gold will be the quantity of currency printed. The more currency that is printed, the higher the price for gold since the supply of gold is relatively fixed. The rate of inflation then is the controlling factor in the price of gold.

Is there a logical saturation point with respect to the demand for gold? Since all price equations depend upon both supply and demand is it possible that sales of gold by the U.S. government, South Africa, the International Monetary Fund and others will exhaust the demand? The answer lies in their gold sales over recent years. All such sales have been oversubscribed. Typically the offers to buy have been for three to four times the amount of gold that was offered for sale. In such a situation the demand obviously exceeds the supply. The reasons for the excess demand relate to the need for governments to replenish their gold stock. There is also a worldwide demand from individual buyers who are seeking some form of permanent wealth. The little old Asian lady who buys a half ounce bar is seeking, in her own intuitive way, to protect her meager resources from being eroded by inflation. As long as inflation rages gold will continue to be an attractive hedge against the uncertainties that lie in the future.

What the critics of gold do not seem to understand is that gold is the primary offsetting factor which can protect you from the ravages of inflation. Such critics seem blind to the fact that currency today serves only as a medium of exchange. The critics fail to comprehend the basic deep-seated conservatism in most people which leads them to buy gold, even in very small amounts, not as a means to a quick profit, but as a means to protect and preserve what little wealth they have been able to accumulate.

CHAPTER 5
THE ENERGY CRUNCH

There has always been an energy shortage. Everyone at all times and places has been able to perceive that if he could run faster and farther, or carry more or keep warmer he could do something additional. Man has always had the potential to initiate more activities than he could carry out. The harnessing of sources of energy was therefore one of the first human acts, first as a part of simple survival and later as a means of enhancing his lifestyle. We began as cooperative hunters and gatherers sharing our energy for the good of the group. Our ancestors then forged ahead to new levels of technology with the harnessing of other, nonhuman, sources of energy—fire, domestic animals, the sun to dry and preserve foods, the sun to make salt, the wind to propel boats etc. The shift to fossil fuels gave birth to the industrial revolution. This power could run machines to do tasks previously done by hand. Power was initially provided by wood, then water, wind, coal, petroleum, electricity, and finally nuclear energy. As long as those sources of energy were relatively cheap our use of them and our dependence upon them grew logarithmically—at ever increasing rates. What began as simple became through time complex and changed from attractive options or luxuries to necessities. We have grown to rely on those technological advances to the extent that they are now essential to the survival of our society as we know it. The automobile is no longer a faster replacement for the horse—it is the only way we can get to our place of employment, to the store, doctor, or anywhere else we have to go since the entire transportation system is based on the use of the automobile. We cannot substitute the horse back for the automobile —it simply wouldn't do the job. Think back for a moment to the tiny towns of the 19th century, small towns at three-mile intervals were a convenient horseback ride from the farm home. Larger towns were no more than a half-day's ride away since you often needed to return home the same day. With the advent of the automobile those small towns died. You could drive twenty to thirty miles in an hour, shop and be back home before lunch. Therefore the middle size towns survived. Now that we depend upon the automobile and electrically powered appliances, not only in the home but in industry as well, we can't go back. Our only option is to seek alternative fuels or more efficient ways to use the fuels available in order to preserve our present standard of living without too great a disruption.

Our question then is which options are available to us with respect to the availability of each of the major sources of energy in the foreseeable future? At present, we obtain 96% of our energy needs from only four sources, oil, natural gas, coal and uranium. Given a predicted worldwide shortfall in the production of energy, and the U.S. constituting the world's single greatest consumer of energy, it behooves us to develop as quickly as possible alternative sources of energy. The principal alternatives include oil shale, tar sands, solar power, garbage and crop residues, coal gasification, geothermal energy, hydroelectric power, the wind, and the ocean. The future potential for these alternatives can be great indeed since at present all alternative sources produce only 4% of our current needs. They can only grow in their utility. However, we need more energy now. Therefore we shall explore the potential of these alternative sources to reduce our current shortfall.

Petroleum

Regardless of price the critical element with respect to petroleum is its availability. The availability of known oil reserves for 1979 and 1949 demonstrates that over a thirty year period a great deal of oil exploration has been successful. More than seven times as many reserves are now proven as were known in 1949. Several major facts however stand out. The first is that the known U.S. reserves are approximately the same as they were 30 years ago and that is bad. In not increasing our known reserves over that period the United States has dropped from the position of Number One in known reserves to seventh. A second major fact is that the big producers today, for the most part, were big producers 30 years ago. Of the top nations now producing more than the U.S., only one, the United Arab Emirates, was not a large producer 30 years ago. This fact implies that the major oil reserves of the world are known and have been known for over 30 years. Meanwhile the United States has continued its position as the Number One world user of petroleum.

The only major industrialized nation that exports oil is the former U.S.S.R. All other major world powers are net importers. By contrast the only underdeveloped nations that import oil are Brazil and India. The facts are clear, the haves—the industrialized nations—are paying the have-not nations more than 100 billion dollars per year for oil. Of this total over 40% comes from the United States. This fantastic payoff is the result of the OPEC cartel's control of the world oil price. Between 1973 and 1979 their monopolistic price for crude oil increased almost 6 times from $2.41 to $14.55 per barrel. Today's price is twice that.

Can we look forward to reduced consumption or increased production which will limit our dependence on OPEC oil? It's not likely for a variety of reasons. U.S. consumption is still increasing. The reason for the increase includes more cars and recreational vehicles on our highways, plus more drivers. There are now over 100 million passenger cars in this country, almost one for each two Americans. Federal mileage standards required that passenger cars have a fleet average of 27.5 miles per gallon by 1985. Did we achieve that goal? The improvement in mileage from the introduction of compacts and subcompacts is no cause to cheer. Since establishment of the mileage goals the average mileage has only improved a few miles per gallon. Meanwhile gas guzzling SUVs have dominated the market. Total consumption is still increasing due to more cars on the road. Federal air pollution standards add to the problem since they favor lead free gas. Unleaded requires 10% more crude oil to produce than the leaded version. The only hope for decreased consumption to any major degree would be based on:

1. A dramatic change in driving habits, which is unlikely to occur in spite of increasing gasoline prices. Only strict rationing might have a chance to succeed;

2. Cessation of manufacture of all large gas burning models; or

3. A massive switch to diesel or electric powered automobiles.

In my opinion a combination of a switch to compact gasoline powered cars plus a greater use of diesel or electric cars is the only workable solution. Whether the American public will be willing to make this shift is as yet unclear. One potential breakthrough is the Prius. This is a compact, powered by a gasoline/electric engine which averages 50 miles per gallon. Give some thought to the diesel or electric car in your future. It may be the only way we can reduce our petroleum consumption to a level compatible with world supplies.

OPEC currently supplies over half of the world market. The 13 members of OPEC produce most the world's "surplus oil" available for purchase. This monopoly may be expected to continue since it is unrealistic to expect that either fuel conservation or increased domestic production can improve the situation very much. For example, much of the oil industry's exploratory activities since 1949 have focused on sedimentary basins that were already known prior to that date. Even the North Slope of Alaska, Libya, Oman, and the United Arab Emirates were perceived as having potential for oil development more than 50 years ago. Perhaps the major change since 1949 has been exploration on the continental shelves. However even that source has begun to reach a point of diminishing returns. The expenses are horrendous with an offshore drilling rig costing as much as $230 million. Drilling in the Baltimore canyon area failed to produce any commercial finds even though drilling costs exceeded $400 million. What are the possibilities that we will discover and develop major new petroleum reserves?

Of all the natural resources which the oceans have yielded, perhaps the most vital are oil and gas and it is important to locate and exploit the available reserves ....The North Sea is not at all unique in its development of hydrocarbon reserves. During the past few years increasing interest has been paid to offshore west Greenland, the Barents Sea, and even the Antarctic Ocean. Large coal reserves have been found on the Antarctic mainland. Beneath the great ice cap vast mineral and hydrocarbon reserves may lie waiting to be exploited. If the technology is available to cope with the problem of up to 4,000 metres of mobile ice, these reserves may also be tapped in the years to come (Reynolds, 1978, p.24)

As Reynolds states, the potential is there. However the costs will be enormous and the lead-time required will be substantial. In the meantime we can expect a continuing shortage of oil for the foreseeable future. The graphs below (Figs 11 and 12) give you the picture.

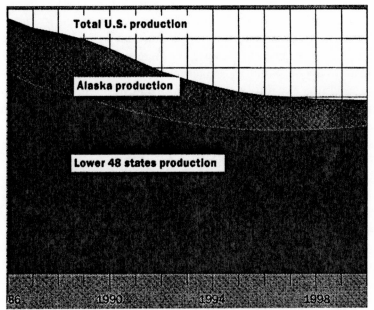

Total U.S. production

Alaska production

Lower 48 states production

86   1990   1994   1998

Figure 11: Declining U.S. Crude Oil Production. From Klott (1990 p. 361)

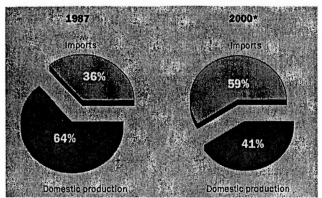

Figure 12: America's Rising Dependence on Imports Share of daily crude oil supply. From Klott (1990 p. 362)

Summary

The energy crunch seems likely to be with us for the foreseeable future. The potential for increased oil production does not appear to be promising and conservation seems to provide only a limited possibility of reducing our shortfall. Estimates of the potential of alternative sources seem to me to be wildly optimistic. Whereas we have been told solar power or increased hydro power or use of wood can provide up to 15% to 20% of our needs in the 21st century, a realistic appraisal seems to be much lower than that. The higher figures are all dependent upon rapid development, Congressional support, tax incentives, and technological breakthroughs. Since these factors have not occurred we can look forward to a continuing energy shortfall since our consumption is still increasing. Meanwhile all other alternative sources, wind sea, etc, can be expected to contribute little until the technology is dramatically improved. Only coal and natural gas seem to have much potential to meet our needs. Given the expectations we believe that the costs of all forms of energy, gasoline, electricity, propane, heating oil, etc. will continue to increase. This is thus an inflationary component in our cost of living which can be expected to consume a greater proportion of our individual and national incomes. The long term net result can be expected to include a reduction in our standard of living and less profitability in all forms of business, both industrial and agricultural. The latter impact over the long term can be expected to be a major cause of the next depression.

CHAPTER 6
THE TAX REVOLT

The Revolt in Payment of Income Taxes

There are those who simply refuse to pay income taxes. They file a blank tax return and for a variety of reasons do not pay any tax. Their case is based on a complex legal background. One gambit is to state that on constitutional grounds the income tax is illegal since the constitution specifically forbids the assessment of any "direct" tax on individuals. Another point of view is that since the constitution defines legal tender in terms of gold and silver, these constitute true money. Therefore as the individual has not received any gold or silver in payment for his services or product, he has not received any "income". According to the tax resisters, the receipt of U.S. greenbacks and copper-nickel clad coins does not meet the constitutionally defined standards of legal tender.

The typical response to those ploys by the IRS is to take the individual to court and get an indictment for "tax evasion" or "nonpayment" of taxes. The real issues have not yet been tested in court and it seems likely that the IRS is not eager to have them resolved by the courts.

There are famous cases of tax resisters. One of the best known is that of Frank McNulty who won $128,410 in the Irish Sweepstakes in 1973. He deposited $100,000 in Irish pounds in a bank on the Isle of Jersey where they are earning 9%. He claims that since the money was earned outside the U.S. and never brought in to this country, his winnings are not taxable in this country. The IRS contends that the earnings of a U.S. citizen living in this country are taxable no matter where they were obtained. What is most unique is that at the time the IRS presented McNulty with three different tax bills: $75,000, $83,000 and $89,000. This question has never been adequately answered. On what basis did the IRS compute three bills? Surely, given the normal course of human affairs, at least two of those bills were in error. The question is, which two? Meanwhile McNulty refused to pay any taxes at all and the U.S. government could not legally attach his funds in another country. As a result he was tried and convicted for tax evasion and sentenced to five years in prison. Unrepentant, he served four years, one month and eight days before being paroled. What also matters to you as a citizen is the treatment that McNulty received. He claims he was shadowed for over a year by IRS agents before his arrest. At the time of his arrest he was pounced upon in his home, by armed IRS agents who were without a warrant for his arrest. In McNulty's terms he was kidnapped and then handcuffed and dragged to their car. The case is not resolved legally and one can assume that if McNulty is able to leave the country he can live tax free with his assets on the Isle of Jersey. An associated problem is that he has little chance of obtaining a passport from the State Department, therefore he would have to flee the country as a common criminal.

What is significant to our discussion here is that the tax revolt is growing and its increase is directly related to increases in inflation and in income taxes assessed. As the tax revolt grows in future years the possibility of non-payment of U.S. governmental obligations increases as well.

Barter—The Poor Man's Friend

Barter is an archaic economic system which depends upon the exchange of goods and services. No currency or money of any form is involved. The barterers simply agree between themselves that a fair exchange consists of two chickens for a bushel of potatoes or whatever other items they have to trade. The concept is simple, you trade whatever you have in excess for someone else's excess goods. A variant is where you trade your services. You agree to paint your neighbor's garage or whatever. However more sophisticated bartering is in effect today, largely as a result of our tax structure. A lawyer friend of ours is an example. We shall call him the Legal Eagle, since he is busy clipping the wings off the IRS without their knowledge. He routinely accepts items in trade for his services from his clients. He does their legal work in exchange for whatever excess items they have. A TV set, a motorcycle, a stereo, a pickup with camper, are his now to possess—largely through his skill the IRS to finesse. A part-time plumber I know sells antiques, guns, and coins on the side and has indicated that he is also willing to trade. When he fixed our plumbing he accepted cash, but at a rate less than union scale.

Viewed in this context barter is a part of the underground economy and probably it is not possible to separate the cash transactions from those conducted in exchange for goods or services. In any event the Barter System is truly the poor man's friend since it enables him to get what he wants without having to pay taxes first and then end up with only half of what he wants or needs.

Corporations have joined the barter game as well. The annual total volume of such business is now estimated at $15 billion so it is not chickenfeed. The estimate is that 60% of all companies on the New York Stock Exchange engage in barter. Often the items bartered are not saleable at retail or even cost so barter permits a corporation to exchange its dead inventory for items it would otherwise have had to buy.

The lesson for those who pass and enforce our tax laws is that excessive taxation reduces the value of currency and penalizes legitimate transactions for cash. Often the tax savings effected through barter spell the difference between staying in business and operating at a profit, versus losing money on every transaction. A further word to the taxing authorities is that as they increase taxes they make barter transaction more attractive. Since barter avoids taxes it is a powerful counterforce which the taxers would be wise not to encourage. In short, my recommendation to them is to be careful not to increase taxes since such action could make it more difficult to collect taxes that are already assessed.

The Underground Economy

The majority of the participants in the underground economy are salaried employees who augment their regular income which is directly taxed through payroll deductions, through a wide variety of part-time activities which are paid for in cash. Those involved claim that they participate in the underground economy to "make ends meet" or to "give them something to do." They don't view it as "work," but consider it more as a "hobby." Nonetheless the number of persons involved is in the millions. According to the U.S. Congress Joint Economic Committee (1980) who have studied the phenomenon, the total sum involved is in the order of 200 billion dollars each year. That seems like a lot to spend on baby-sitting, lawn care, car washing, house painting, plumbing repairs, electrical and cement contracting as well as purchases made at garage sales, flea markets, coin shows, etc. That fact suggests that the unemployment rate published by the government is too high. If we take into account underground employment then the unemployment roster might be as much as 1.6 million less individuals listed as unemployed. The tax consequences are also significant, as unreported income means non-taxed income. The IRS has done its own study of the underground economy and states that unreported income is closer to 100 billion annually. Gutmann bases his figures on the discrepancy between the amount of money in circulation and the amount of money in checking and savings accounts. The difference, which is the amount of money in the underground economy can be accounted for in several ways. Organized crime makes up a substantial portion with cash being used for gambling and drug transactions. Another factor is the amount of cash that people are hoarding. These underground activities have led to the $100 bill dilemma. With 290 million $100 bills printed and in circulation, why do we rarely see one used in our daily transactions? Since 1960 the number of $100 bills has more than doubled. Yet with credit cards and widespread acceptance of checks there is little seeming rationale for the use of two to three times as many century notes. The Congressional Report states that unaccounted for cash in circulation is $85 billion, which amounts to $1,545 for each American (U.S. Congress Joint Economic Committee 1980). Do you have your share stashed at home, if not, where is all that cash? Some experts believe that numbers of individuals are stuffing their mattresses with cash as a form of saving for a rainy day. The primary reason cited for this behavior is a distrust of banks. If we are to believe this line of reasoning then approximately one half of the entire population doesn't believe banks are safe. Somehow I doubt that explanation. On the other hand there is a clear need for large amounts of cash for transactions conducted for criminal purposes. I am sure that drug payoffs and other criminal activities can account for perhaps $20 billion per year (this is an unsubstantiated guess) but that would still leave $65 billion in the hands of ordinary Americans. It is my point of view that most of this cash is kept for underground transactions which are primarily conducted as a means of avoiding taxation. The average man on the street calls it "making ends meet" and it consists of moonlighting for additional income which is received in cash and never declared on one's income tax return. In that manner a relatively few additional hours work per week can supplement a paycheck already ravaged by taxes withheld. In fact Eliot Janeway (1979) states that this is the *only* way the average individual can keep up with inflation, by moonlighting and then using that untaxed income to pay off his bills. This additional income goes twice as far since if declared it would be taxed at the highest rate the individual would pay. When not declared it's all "spending money." The individuals involved when interviewed say they are paying sufficient taxes and what they need is some additional cash on hand to offset the effects of inflation.

Do not be misled by those who claim that most of the excess cash in circulation is simply being hoarded. Polls have demonstrated that 40% of all households utilize the services of those in the underground economy. At the local flea market a typical Saturday turns up several hundred sellers, many of whom are not clearing out their garages, but are selling merchandise they have purchased for resale. What they sell includes fruit and vegetables with a short storage life expectancy, discount jeans such a factory seconds, T-shirts, shoes, canned goods, as well as a wide variety of manufactured consumer items like tires, auto parts, tape decks, VCR's, computers, tools etc. These items may have been purchased from either discount wholesalers or from fire sales or firms going out of business. In any case the sellers have an advantage over regular merchants since they have minimal overhead and pay no taxes.

I consider the underground economy to be a part of the tax revolt even if others chose to label it with other names. To put it in other terms, the underground economy, with the exception of the criminal portion, is a direct result of two major influences on the average American family—inflation and taxes. I further believe that such practices will continue and will increase until the taxpayer receives a reduction in his tax bill.

The Overpayment Problem

Did you ever have the feeling when computing your income taxes that the forms are unduly complex? Did you ever wonder that you didn't know how much income tax you really owed? Have you ever used the services of a tax accountant only to learn that he missed an obvious deduction? Have you ever disagreed with your tax accountant over whether a specific item was deductible or not? If you have had any of these experiences then you and I have a common experience we can share.

I have also, back in the days when my income was about at today's legal poverty level, spent an entire weekend computing my taxes on the long form, taking all the deductions permissible, only to learn that I would get back $10 more if I utilized the short form. As a result of all of these enjoyable and enlightening experiences, it is now my view that all you need to compute your taxes these days is a degree in tax accounting. Meanwhile what does this state of affairs bode for the average American crumb winner? It is my opinion that most Americans overpay their income taxes simply because they cannot understand the complexities of the system. I know of no studies on this topic so can only guess. However it would not surprise me if the total overpayment of taxes is in the vicinity of 10%. Several factors can cause over payment:

1. Failure to file for a rebate.

2. Failure to claim deductions legally allowable.

3. Failure to correctly compute tax owed.

4. A mistaken view of patriotism which leads to deliberate overpayment.

5. Errors made by one's tax accountant.

In any case once overpaid those funds remain the property of the government. A further gripe is that the forms are so complex, as a result of our incredibly complex tax code, that you cannot fill them out without assistance. This is a tax in itself since you are forced to pay an accountant simply to ensure that: 1) Your return is properly and legally computed, and 2) You received the deductions that you are legally entitled to. An analogy which comes to mind, albeit not too good a one, is having to dig your own grave.

No matter what the reason for overpayment of taxes just remember the government has had the use of your excess taxes at no cost and without justification.

The Property Tax Revolt

Passage of the Jarvis-Gann Amendment (Proposition 13) in California during the summer of 1978 posed a severe threat to the existence of government as we have come to know it in the last several decades. For the first time the voters united in the face of total governmental opposition, to throw off the yoke of financial servitude that had been placed upon them by their quote—chuckle "leaders." Suddenly there loomed the possibility of a society governed by the people without coercion from their self-selected political mentors. The consequences were almost beyond comprehension. Would the schools be shut down, would the fire department and police be added to the welfare roles? And were the welfare programs themselves in danger? What would the unemployed politicians do? They are ill prepared for productive employment and just as they would be thrust out of a job—the welfare programs would be curtailed!

In my opinion the politicians overreacted having failed to understand the underlying causes of the revolt. The basic thrust of the amendment was not so much a blow at the power of the politicians to tax, as it was an expression of frustration at being unable to control inflation, especially in the area of housing costs. The message to the politicians was clear—do not increase taxes beyond our ability to pay. The majority of city, county, and special district programs that were in effect in California have continued. The cessation of services in a gigantic collapse as predicted by local politicians prior to the Proposition 13 election has not occurred.

The tax revolt, with all of its manifestations, may be perceived as primarily a revolt against the effects of inflation. Only secondarily is it a revolt against the government's right to impose taxes in order to provide essential services. The fact that inflation itself is a hidden form of taxation is not perceived by the common man. If we can predict the future then: as inflation increases objections to specific forms of taxes will increase. As these objections increase there will be an associated increase in the number of people who question the government's authority to tax. The solutions seem equally simplistic: reduce inflation and the tax revolt will fade away.

CHAPTER 7
THE DECLINE AND FALL OF
THE AMERICAN EMPIRE

Social Security—Panacea or Placebo?

The late breaking news which isn't news any longer is that the Social Security system is in trouble. Over the past four decades attitudes toward the system that was first viewed with skepticism have changed to wide acceptance and endorsement of this program for old age subsistence. Only in the late 20th century has the fiscal base of the program been revealed to be shaky. The problems are both the result of inflation and changes in the demographic makeup of the population. Strictly speaking, the program is neither an insurance plan nor an annuity. Payments made are not held in any form for the future use of those paying. Payments made are immediately paid out to current pensioners. This means that as future wage earners change in numbers relative to the number of pensioners they must pay more or less as the ratio of wage earners to pensioners changes. The current trends are worrisome since pensioners are living longer at the same time that wage earners are retiring earlier. Further the decline in the birthrate has the social security actuaries seriously worried about the future viability of the program. Currently there are five workers for each social security recipient but future projections show that ratio declining to three to one by the year 2030. The Medicare portion of the program is in even greater difficulty with that program estimated as being bankrupt in the near future. Solutions to this problem can only be provided by a reduction in the rate of inflation, a reduction in the rate of unemployment, a increase in the birth rate—leading to more tax paying workers, or an increase in worker productivity—making it possible to make up the deficit through increased withholding taxes.

Solutions which have been proposed in Congress include allocation of other federal tax monies, derived from income taxes, or the proposed new value added tax. Finally is the proposal that social security taxes be invested in the stock market. None of these proposals has strong support at present, especially the latter since the stock market crash of 2000-2002. At the moment there is only a faint possibility that payroll deductions will be reduced from current levels since any cut in social security tax rates would threaten to bankrupt the entire system sooner. Raising rates is also not likely due to the already too high burden of taxes on the individual. It is a true dilemma which to date appears to be insoluable.

Meanwhile everyone agrees that there is no way that the government will substantially alter the program to reduce benefits. The program is so basic a cornerstone of our welfare state that no politician would risk antagonizing the entire voting public. No one wants the program to end, however, the march of demographic changes plus inflation may well end it for us whether we want that to happen or not. Current baby boomers in the work force worry that by the time they retire the social security welfare net will be empty.

The Current Real Estate Boom

Some are predicting that a crash in the single family housing market is just around the corner. They claim that similarities exist between earlier booms and present day conditions. The reason is the existence of a speculative boom in real estate prices. A speculative boom may be defined as the result of paying a premium for something in the expectation of growth in its value. In the case of a boom the growth assumption which may have been justified for a variety of reasons in early years is gradually replaced by higher and higher prices which are merely the result of the expectation of higher prices in the future. Once the cycle proceeds to a point where price increases are not matched by increased production of income then the boom has become speculative in nature. The public at large may still be unaware that a boom is in progress. They accept the speculative potential as justified fact. Prices have gone up in the recent past therefore they will continue to go up in the future. Such booms have been typical in all times and places, but their occurrence is spaced widely enough in time that each comes to a new generation and is normally in a new form. Past examples include the Tulip craze of 17th century Holland, the South Sea Bubble in England, the Chicago Real Estate boom of the 1830's, the Florida Land boom in the 1920's, the Stock Market boom of 1926-1929, and many others.

These increases in price have convinced many Americans to buy now since they fear that to wait would mean they would forever be unable to catch up with the price escalator. So far their reasoning has been correct. By now the boom has lasted so long, more than a single generation, that bankers and other lenders have become convinced as well and are liberalizing their lending rules so that those with lower incomes relative to the monthly payments are being approved for loans. The former rules were that no lender would approve a loan for a house costing more than twice the family's annual income or with payments exceeding 25% of monthly income. Today's home buyers may commit 30% to 40% of their income for housing costs. Both buyers and lenders cite the growth expectation as one reason for the lowering of lending requirements; another supportive factor is the tax saving from the deduction of interest payments.

The average homebuyer is not aware that he is speculating. Such opinions have been rampart in all past booms as well. In the current craze the justification is that if you plan to occupy the home then you are not a speculator. The truth is that at present the costs of home ownership exceed the costs of renting, even taking into account the tax savings. Therefore for the homebuyer to do well the future price must increase—in short, a speculative anticipation—the single common element in all booms. It must also be pointed out here that the increase in single family housing has exceeded the rate of inflation. Whereas the genesis of the growth anticipation lies in inflation, the growth in home prices has now come to generate its own excesses. The boom is now self feeding and will continue until a combination of factors brings about a crash in prices. Such factors are already apparent. They include:

1.   Rental units generating negative cash flow.

2.   Home ownership is more costly than renting.

3.   Owing to increased prices the number of families that can afford a new home has been cut in half.

4.   The peak in birth rates was in 1958 and is now 25% below that figure. Therefore:

     a. Demand for housing is expected to peak soon.

     b. With smaller families we will see a trend to smaller homes.

Your house is a major portion of your net worth so can you sit idly by and watch that value be cut in half when the crash in prices comes?

How Bad is Housing Inflation Right Now?

Everyone knows that housing prices are high. Just how high requires some analysis. For example, we purchased a 3 bedroom, 2 bathroom, brick rambler with a finished basement on a 1/4th acre lot in a Washington, D.C. suburb in July of 1978. The house was 27 years old and had cost about $15,000 when it was new. Built according to a standardized plan, it was identical to every other house on the same block. Our purchase price was $76,000. We sold the house ten months later for $89,000, a gross profit of $13,000, a 17% increase. We used a G.I. loan for the purchase so no down payment was necessary. The mortgage was for a 30-year term at 9.5% interest with a total payment of $739 a month of which $38 represented repayment of the principal. Paid out to maturity, the total price over 30 years would have totaled $225,000. Since it took four months for the G.I. loan to clear we only made six payments. Our equity represented by principal that had been paid off was only $228! At the same time inflation caused the price of that same house to move up a total of $1,300 per month, almost twice the monthly payment! At the time we sold the local real estate agents told us our house was actually priced below the market as they had similar units priced up to $95,000. What concerns me is that the march of inflation has caused such a deal to be common practice. The increase in equity we recovered was 98.3% due to inflation and 1.7% due to repayment of principal borrowed. A more up to date example concerns a house in Denver purchased by our son in December 1988. Using an FHA loan his down payment was minimal, $2,000. The purchase price was $76,500. Last week the house was appraised at $245,000. The inflationary increase in value is approximately 220% over a 13-year term, or 16.9% per year. Can such increases be expected to continue?* Surely the buyer who buys into such an inflationary market runs a tremendous speculative risk. Inflation may continue at high levels and he may sell out at a profit. But sooner or later the last buyer will be facing 30 years of high payments in a time of depression. At that point 30 years will seem like a very long time indeed.

The Environmental Bind

Environmental groups stress the values of preservation of native habitat, spawning grounds, and wildlife. Where those values are considered to be paramount the development of minerals, timber, etc. on those lands is accorded a secondary priority. Since much development is detrimental to environmental values our Congress and the federal agencies are engaged in a massive effort to assign priorities. In short they must make difficult choices with high associated long-term costs. Ten years ago approximately 17% of all federal lands were restricted to economic development. Today that figure is close to 60%. Whereas the eventual result may be that some lands now restricted to development will be reopened, the current shutdown has negatively affected mining, lumbering, and other natural resource industries.

No matter what your political views on the issue whether you favor more environmental preservation or more development, the result will be the same for each of us: higher prices due to shortages of critical materials. These include coal, gas, oil, molybdenum, copper, zinc, lead, gold, silver, firewood, lumber, plywood, plastics, electrical power, fertilizer, etc. Our concern for the quality of the environment has therefore become another inflationary impact on our standard of living.

---

*By contrast the official cumulative rate of inflation since 1982-84 in all consumer items is 81.3% *(Wall Street Journal* Nov. 20, 2002) or 4% per year.

Whatever Happened to the Tooth Fairy?

Remember when you were a kid and you placed your tooth under your pillow? The tooth was extracted after much wiggling back and forth, or the painless way—tied to a string attached to the doorknob. To your amazement the next morning there was a dime, or a quarter, in place of the tooth. The money was all yours, to spend as you wished. Today, somehow, it all seems different. The reason is that the tooth fairy is dead, having been murdered by inflation. No longer will a dime, or even a quarter bring delight to the average six year old. The problem is that you can no longer buy anything special with any of our current coins. It would take at least $5.00 to evoke enthusiasm from today's inflation scarred six year old. Meanwhile, something similar has happened to the adults in our society as well. My mother tells of the time in her youth when an evening's entertainment consisted of young people getting together to perform amateur minstrel shows and to dance to their own musical accompaniment. The cost was zero, other than a little hay for the horse or some gas for the Model T. Today it's different, everything has a price tag attached and entertainment especially so. Remember the last time you took your spouse or friend to the movies? The tab looked like this:

2 tickets	$14.00
gas	1.50
parking	5.00
pop corn	3.00
2 cokes	4.00
2 ice cream sundaes after the show	4.50
Total	$33.00

On the other hand what if you went out to dinner and then the theater? Dinner for two at the local Hong Kong Phoey's could easily cost $30.00. While at a better restaurant (one that advertises) $50-$60 would be on target. Theater tickets, for those with binoculars begin at $15 and go on up from there. After lingering over a brandy or two at the after hours club you learn to your surprise that all you have left out of that C note jingles.

What has all of this inflation done to our aspirations and expectations? We no longer feel free to do something for others without charging. Further we expect to have to pay for whatever others do for us. Even when they refuse to charge for a favor we feel obligated to buy them a gift. For if we say, "We'll do something for you some day," we run the risk of being considered a cheapskate. In short, one of the consequences of inflation is that people can no longer afford to exchange cooperative services any more. Everyone has unpaid bills and needs to exchange their time for cash to pay those bills.

There is no need to belabor the point. Inflation has changed our daily lifestyles, not only in the cost of items but in our attitudes toward each other. It further has changed our willingness to work. We expect to be paid more for doing less and gripe when our employer expects a day's work for eight hours pay. Even the minimum wage law has its negative side since it discourages employment of teenagers and others who are willing to do odd jobs for less than the legal minimum wage. We further have inflation in everything else; packages are smaller, we have the seven and eleven ounce beers, and the small candy bar in the large wrapper. Even college grades are inflated, a C is no longer the average grade, if you don't get a B you feel discriminated against. Class hours in attendance are reduced but not the hours credit granted. The list seems endless.

Whereas we recognize that these attitudes are current we must also recognize that in the long run they are counterproductive and based on inflationary expectations. Therefore, we must change our attitudes since, as a nation, we cannot consume more than we produce and work is necessary in order to produce anything. That is the lesson from the Tooth Fairy.

What Does the Future Hold?

Prognosticators of the future, called prophets by some, and false prophets by others, spell out their views in unilateral terms. "Such and such *is* going to happen". In reality unforeseen events may make their predictions unrealizable in part or in whole. Therefore it seems best to present more than one scenario. For example, C.V. Myers (1976) has stated that we will drift or slide into a depression without an intervening phase between now and then of runaway inflation. Some anticipate runaway inflation. Others have been predicting the crash for years. My concern is not so much in attempting to predict specific future events but to outline in general what may occur. If we understand how such events occur we are thereby better prepared to cope with them whatever they may be.

The political and economic situation seems to be serious, therefore, at this time it seems appropriate to emulate Churchy in Pogo who states: "You look puzzle. Mebbe my fresh young brain kin help on account I ain't used it today"(Kelly 1979, p. 120). The question, of course, is which of these current events have significance for the long term and what direction will future events take? What will happen of course no one knows. All I can do here is summarize the nature of current events as I have related them in this study so far. In brief, these major factors suggest the following conditions for the future:

1. Owing to the price of imported oil the dollar will continue to be pressured downward on the international currency market.

2. We will continue to have an energy crisis with oil increasing in price and all alternative sources of energy will be both expensive to develop and will require long periods of time for development.

3. Energy conservation will have a record of minimal success.

4. The Tax Revolt will continue and maybe will intensify affecting a broader spectrum of taxpayers.

5. The cost price squeeze on agricultural producers will continue.

6. Our Balance of Payments will continue to be negative and our federal deficit will increase.

7. Fine tuning of the economy will continue to be unsuccessful in keeping the unemployment rate and the inflation rate at target levels.

8. All of the non-productive federal services, welfare, regulation of industry, environmental protection, military pre-

paredness, pensions, etc will continue to pose a massive inflationary pressure on the entire economy.

9.   The social security system will become increasingly unstable from a fiscal standpoint.

10.   Union demands will continue to be inflationary.

11.   The real estate market will become even more speculative.

12.   Owing to taxing problems, plus inflationary increases in costs, municipal and state governments will have difficulty balancing their budgets.

All of the above trends are in effect today. The only degree of prediction of the future that I have employed is to assume that these trends will continue and that, primarily because of inflation they will intensify.

If my predictions are on target we can move forward in our analysis to examine what you can do to prepare for the difficult times ahead.

PART IV

WHAT YOU CAN DO TO PREPARE FOR THE FUTURE

We perceive two major possibilities for the future, continuing inflation, and a crash followed by a depression. The course of these events is not under our control nor seemingly under the control of our government. I expect their efforts to "fine tune" the economy to be too little, too late, and largely ineffective. This leaves the brunt of whatever is to come to be borne by you, the average American. The time to take action is now, prior to the arrival of those events. We have seen in our historical review that times past the common people were largely helpless in their efforts to survive during the times of major adversity. Further and this is most significant, their governments were not only helpless but incapable of taking any corrective actions. Often the actions taken by the government seemed to add to the problem. For example, Herbert Hoover has written that Roosevelt's New Deal didn't end the depression or solve the social problems, World War II did (Hoover, 1952). This means that in times of future crises you must have your own solution already worked out and between now and then you must prepare so that you can put those solutions into effect when the time comes. You may rest assured that most people will not prepare and they will be caught totally by surprise when the rug is pulled out. What can *you* do to prepare for the future? In the first place this book is written on the assumption that you are an average American. This assumes that you have a salaried job, that you own your home but have a substantial mortgage left to pay, that you have in addition, credit cards and other current debts, and that you do not have a substantial amount of savings or other investments. You are not an inheritor and if you lost your job you would have difficulty meeting your expenses within 30 to 60 days. Sound familiar? If this is the boat that you are in then this section of the book is for you. Several items stand out as preparation for the future. Learn to cut your living costs, learn some additional skills that could bring in additional income, especially if you lost your job, and begin *now* a systematic financial plan for the tough times ahead.

CHAPTER 8
WHAT ARE YOUR DEGREES
OF FREEDOM OR A COGIS
NOTA WHEEL

Numerous works have covered the topic of preparing yourself for future financial emergencies. Without seeking to
discredit those authors, the average financial preparedness book stresses financial solutions. One is advised to shift one's
assets from real estate to foreign bonds or from stocks to gold,
etc. The basic assumption is that by doing so you will be protected
against financial crises. What we have learned from our historical
review is that these crises, such as hyperinflation or a depression,
are not only financial crises; they are social crises as well. The
financial advice books also assume that you have a lot of assets to
protect. We know better; even with the rapid escalation in home
prices, the average middle class American has net assets of less
than $100,000, often much less. Owing to our tax structure, plus
inflation, it is possible to make a high salary and still have difficulty
accumulating any real wealth. Assets of the average American
minus mortgages and consumer debt frequently equal zilch.
Therefore the primary problem faced by many Americans in the
future is not protecting their assets but protecting their lifestyle.
This is what I mean by the title "a cog is not a wheel". If you have
lots of real estate, stocks, or bonds, or bags of gold and silver this
book won't help you much. This book is intended to help those

who, if they lost their job could lose everything they own. If that is your situation than you may not be free to take Howard Ruff's (1979) advice and sell your present urban or suburban home and move to a small town where things are cheaper. If you cannot find an equal job elsewhere then you have to work out your own preparedness plan right where you are. What are your degrees of freedom? Can you find equal employment elsewhere in an area with a cheaper cost of living? Can you cut your present living costs? Can you develop auxiliary skills to either cut costs or augment your income? How secure is your present job? If you lost your present job what could you do? If hyperinflation comes do you have a plan to take advantage of it? If a depression comes do you have a survival plan?

Complacency is the adversary to planning. As long as things seem to be going along reasonably well why not emulate Alfred E. Newman, "What, me worry?" We have seen in our historical review that things were often much worse then they seemed at the time. Meanwhile the political leaders were publicly affirming that conditions were fundamentally sound or had even passed the point where anyone would ever have to worry again. According to their pronouncements the business cycle had been replaced with prosperity forever! The politicians were wrong but it was the people who suffered. In this time when we have the problems of an energy shortage, continuing inflation, a huge federal debt, deficit spending, plus lots of people losing their jobs, a survival plan for the future for each individual seems prudent and wise.

A Plan for Action is Better than Being Guillotine Fodder

We have determined that your degrees of freedom are limited. You can't simply sell everything you own, put your assets into Swiss bonds and live off the proceeds in some low cost retirement utopia. You have to fight it out where you are come what may. In that situation a plan for action is even more important. You must maximize whatever advantages you have so that while others may be selling everything they own at bankruptcy auctions you will at least be able to survive. In order to survive you must have a plan. Foremost among the items on your plan is the security of your present job. If you have any doubts about the future of your position or your ability to keep that job, now is the time to either obtain additional training, look elsewhere, or take other action.

How Secure is Your Job?

A simple first step is to analyze your job as to whether it is essential or not. If essential, you produce a product or a service that people can't do without. For example, if you sell groceries, mine coal, repair automobiles, etc., then even though your salary may take a cut, you will probably stay employed. On the other hand if you are a salesperson in real estate, or work in a frisbee or water ski factory, what you do may be judged superfluous in a financial slowdown. During the 1974-1975 recession those who were hardest hit by unemployment were those on hourly wages, those employed part time, workers under age 25, those paid a straight sales commission, and workers in tourism related jobs (Flanigan 1979, p. 81-81). Today the unemployed include tele-communications workers and computer programmers. According to Time Magazine October 14, 2002 p.52-54 those unemployed in 2002 total 1.6 million, up 93% from 2001. Of these 48% are white-collar workers. That's the change this time around, half of those pounding the pavement looking for jobs are professionals with degrees. At present the total number of unemployed is 8.2 million and the number is still increasing. Another casualty is the job related bonus so if you have built such bonuses into your permanent budget you should rethink that situation. Another clue to evaluating your chance of losing your job concerns whether your region depends on a single industry. In single industry towns the unemployment rate may well exceed the national average.

What is relevant here is to review your present job security, your income, your debt load, and your cost of living. Then on the basis of that information you can begin preparing your action plan. You already know where you are on the totem pole economically in a time of inflation. In a time of deflation, which few people are old enough today to remember, your salary might buy more than it does now. The following list provides salaries of the 1932-1934 era by profession. The dollar amounts are not as important as the relative ranking by profession.

Where was your present profession on the 1932-34 list? Was it near the top, middle, or bottom? Your relative buying power may change for the better or worse should a depression ensue. As a college professor my salary rank was at the lower end of white-collar salaries. In the depression it ranked sixth, right behind doctors, which is a lot better than today's ranking.

1932-1934 Salaries by Profession (Time Life *1969, p. 24)*

U.S. Congressman	$8,663
Airline Pilot	8,000
Railroad Executive	5,064
Lawyer	4,218
Doctor	3,382
College Teacher	3,111
Railroad Conductor	2,729
Police Chief(City of 30,000+)	2,636
Engineer	2,520
Dentist	2,391
Mayor (City of 30,000+)	2,317
Fire chief (City of 30,000+)	2,075
Statistician	1,820
Electrical Worker	1,559
Apartment Superintendent	1,500
Pharmaceutical Salesman	1,500
Bus Driver	1,373
Civil Service Employee	1,284
Public School Teacher	1,227
Registered nurse	936
Stenographer/Bookkeeper	936
Department Store Model	936
Construction Worker	907
Priest	831
Dressmaker	780
Housemother Boys' School	708
Coal Miner	723
Chauffeur	624
Typist	530
Waitress	520
Textile Worker	435
Steel Worker	422
Maid	260
Farm Hand	216

Another way to estimate your future job earnings is to examine how the industry in which you work fared in the depression.

Workers producing shoes had little loss in income or at least kept on working. Those in heavy industry were mostly laid off since reductions in smelting, locomotive production, etc., ranged from 60% to 80%.

Only a few industries did not suffer major declines and those were primarily producing necessary items such as clothing and shoes. Most manufacturing was in a 30% to 40% slump and factories manufacturing heavy machinery and products for new construction were almost totally shut down. The U.S. GNP dropped 30.4% between 1929 and 1933 (Chandler 1970, p. 22).

Industry	Percentage Decline 1929-1933
Shoe production	3.4
Textiles and products	6.4
Cigarette production	6.6
Leather and products	7.4
Gasoline production	7.4
Woolen & worsted cloth production	7.7
Cotton consumption	11.4
Tobacco products	16.7
Manufactured food products	17.8
Cigar production	34.4
Tire and tube production	34.8
Polished plate glass production	42.7
Ship building	53.1
Furniture production	55.6
Nonferrous metals and products	55.9
Lumber production	57.9
Iron and steel	59.3
Machinery	61.6
Cement production	63.1
Nonferrous metal smelting	63.5
Transportation equipment	64.2
Automobile production	65.0
Railroad car production	73.6
Copper production	78.9
Common and face brick production	83.3
Locomotive production	86.4

(Chandler 1970, p. 23)

By industry the drop in income between 1929 and 1933 ranged from zero for government to 80.2% for contracting. All industries averaged a drop in income of 54.3%.

The only persons not suffering a loss of income were government employees. All others had to make do with less and in many cases the reduction in income, even for the employed, amounted to 50% to 70%. Take a good look at your present budget and estimate what you could afford on 50% of your present income. Given your present indebtedness could you still make it or would you be bankrupt? Even though depression prices were lower than 1929 prices, for example, you could buy a new car for $500 to $1,000 and used cars were $50-$60, a modern six room house was $2,800, and food was much cheaper—sirloin steak being 29 cents a pound (Time Life 1969, p. 27). The problem for many was not in buying new items but paying off the mortgages they already had. Finally, as you know, the mortgage default rate rose above 60% in some cities. Further, even though food prices were cheap, many had no income at all. If your present budget were reduced and you couldn't meet all of your present monthly payments and expenses, which items would you give up? Once you have established what you would give up, now is the time to either sell that item and reduce your debt load, or sell something else to reduce your debt load, or give up some of your leisure time activities that cost money but produce no useful product. This is the beginning of your survival plan; review all of your assets and liabilities, current expenditures, needs and wants and begin to plan which ones you can eliminate to either reduce your debts or increase your disposable income.

For example, a couple of weeks ago we went to a moving sale in the local expensive subdivision. The houses are individually designed on one or two acre lots. The owners at the moving sale were selling their, essentially new, fishing equipment, skis, camping equipment, pickup truck with camper, furniture, and household items. They may have been selling only one jump ahead of foreclosure or they may have had a plan to reduce their indebtedness voluntarily. In any event, and this is the main point, most of those items they were selling were both expensive and contributed nothing to their family income or subsistence. These are the kinds of items, with the exception of the fishing equipment, to get rid of while you can still sell them for a good price.

Having a plan for action is therefore your first step in preparing for future events. Essential to that plan is to be prepared mentally, our next section.

Be Prepared Mentally

The greatest trauma experienced during the depression was that of trained individuals who lost their jobs and then found no one wanted their services. They were simply unprepared for the shock of being deemed superfluous by the society. Bankers, accountants, druggists, stock brokers, real estate salesmen, teachers, the list is endless, ended up picking peaches, selling apples on street corners, running Mom and Pop groceries, working in filling stations, etc., whatever they could get, and for many all they could get was federal relief. Our society today is even more vulnerable to this kind of situation. Since we have had almost universal higher education since World War II, we have millions of over trained specialists whose only skills lie in one narrowly defined discipline. The 1974-1975 turndown saw thousands of engineers out of work with nowhere to go. Some were unemployed for two years while others went into farming and other areas and left engineering altogether. Today the unemployed include hundreds of thousands from the Telecommunication and Information Age industries.

Mental preparedness consists of facing squarely the idea that you could lose your job. Once you have accepted that potential catastrophe you are free to plan how to augment your skills so that loss of your present job could be cushioned by a shift to other sources of income. A shift which you become trained for in advance of the time when you may need those new skills.

What If You Lose Your Job?

Being laid off, whether you are individually selected, or a member of a group, is one of the most traumatic things that can happen to anyone. It seems as though your entire life has come to an end and you don't know which way to turn. Actually, career counselors know there are lots of things you can do. The first is to prepare yourself if you know that a layoff is coming. Most people hang on, hoping against hope that they won't be among the ones laid off. Meanwhile time passes and when the day comes they are still unprepared for the next step. Half the battle is won when you accept the fact that you will have to change employment. Then you can begin making contingency plans and learning new skills.

In simple order the steps to take are:

1. Don't panic—face your job loss as simply another problem to be solved.

2. Break the news to your family. It could be the best thing that ever happened to you since it provides an opportunity to review your skills and lifetime goals. After all, the job you lost may have lacked promotional possibilities or other limitations. It certainly didn't provide a continuing permanent source of income. Therefore being in the job market might provide an opportunity to land a better job, start your own business, develop a new skill.

3. Make financial plans for the time you will be unemployed.

4. Borrow money if necessary to tide you over between jobs.

5. Make out a new budget in order to cut expenses. Experts suggest you may be unemployed one week for each thousand dollars of your present income. For example, if you were earning $40,000 per year, it could take you 40 weeks to line up a comparable job.

6. Apply for unemployment insurance, severance pay, sick leave and other benefits. If in fact you have been thinking of a career change, unemployment payments which average 26 weeks are the best way there is to tide you over while you are obtaining additional training or beginning your own business in the basement. You may also be eligible to tap into your pension plan.

7. Review your credentials and assets. Prepare a resume of your skills.

8. Carry out a consistent plan to acquire those new skills you have isolated as necessary to your future career goals. If you cannot acquire them in a formal training course a good alternative is to read everything on the subject at the local library.

9. Recognize that the official employment agencies are less useful to you the farther you are up the career ladder.

They may have a number of positions for beginning accountants but few for corporate treasurers.

10.   Recognize that most of your competition will have training similar to your own. Therefore, you must work on developing and emphasizing a unique approach. What can you do that the others can't?

11.   Develop a flexible approach—consider any reasonable opportunity. Do not kill chances by aiming at too narrow a target.

12.   Recognize that what you must do is to merchandize yourself. It is a selling job and you must work at presenting your skills in the most favorable way possible. After all x number of years experience in x field is not in itself a unique asset; lots of others probably have similar experience. Further simply taking training courses in another or related field is also not an automatic surefire job lander. What is of utmost importance is to identify what your potential employer *needs* that you and hopefully *only you* can provide.

Perhaps you don't really want a salaried job anyway! Most jobs are 9 to 5 with limited vacations and fringe benefits. The work may be boring and promotional opportunities may be minimal. What you may prefer is to develop your own individual career as a consultant or other self-employed specialist. Perhaps you have a unique skill which you can market to a number of employers on your own terms. Give it some thought.

If you go the standard job seeking route you identify prospective employers and send them a copy of your resume and a cover letter outlining your special interest and qualifications. If successful in attracting their interest you will be invited for an interview. Once at the interview you may find they don't really want you for variety of reasons including the possibility that they have already selected another applicant.

What you must do is to be totally prepared for the interview when it is scheduled. Research the employer and find out what they need and above all be calm and present your qualifications in their best light. Don't be afraid to make demands which are appropriate to someone of your status. Point out how your demands will improve the quality of the work to be performed. Do not make impossible or egotistical demands or meekly accept working conditions or prerequisites not appropriate to one with your experience and status. Prior to the interview ask yourself the question what is it that you can do for them. Then in the interview tell them what you can do.

In selecting employers to approach you should: read the wants ads, use your contacts, surf the Internet, and ask around—who needs what? If that doesn't turn up any leads you can advertise or gain entry through a position as a volunteer.

Once you are offered a job bargain tactfully for salary and fringe benefits. You will never have as much leverage again after you have accepted the position. The better you advance your own cause the more respect your employer will have for you.

Remember there are three million more trained graduating seniors than there are jobs. . Far from leading to achievement of the American Dream, the pursuit of a graduate degree these days may be the surest way of making oneself permanently unemployable. What this situation poses for the future is an inversion of the labor pyramid. No longer are all the unemployed those with limited education. The educated are pounding the pavement as well. Given large number of unemployed college graduates, the competition becomes fierce indeed on the employment front. For those young educated unemployed, the depression is already here.

Finding and getting that job will require that you be better prepared, more assertive, and more creative than the rest of the pack. The rewards go to the swift. By contrast those who are laid off and in the ranks of the unemployed suffer much higher rates of divorce, mental illness, alcoholism, drug abuse, and suicide. The difference between them and you is up to you and is dependent upon how well you are prepared when it becomes necessary to change employment.

Will You Be Able to Retire?

Those in the Baby Boomer generation have a tough time ahead in their efforts to afford retirement. A couple of years ago the majority thought they were well on their way to financial security and early retirement. Today they are looking at a drastically reduced 401K plan at the same time that the future of Social Security looks shaky. The losses in the stock market total 7.7 trillion dollars and consumer debt is up 30% over the last five years (*Time* July 29, 2002). Nearly half of all households saved nothing last year. Something has to give, either high expectations for a retirement lifestyle, dreams of early retirement, or both. One answer is that those over 55 who are still working will continue working after age 65. In the late 90's, 73% of all retirees were retiring early, Assuming that it will take five years or more for the 401K plans to recover their recent losses, it seems guaranteed that in the future workers will be retiring at an older age.

How well are you doing in your preparation for retirement? The following chart from *Money Magazine* (Fall 2002, p.64) gives a comparative standard.

| | YOUR AGE | | | | |
	<35	35-44	45-54	55-64	65+
$25K-$50K	$7,350	$37,275	$72,004	$134,107	$226,600
$50K-$75K	36,025	120,584	167,592	253,675	415,530
$75K-$100K	70,159	177,712	250,675	354,019	584,970
$100K-$125K	100,869	242,191	321,675	432,352	654,500
$125K-$150K	142,708	284,264	374,400	487,275	748,072
$150K-plus	208,500	409,700	523,875	675,030	879,180

Figure 13: Average Retirement Savings by Income and Age

Depression Proof Your Future

In a time of depression your principle needs are:

1.   A continuing income

2.   Income sufficient to meet your mortgage payments

3.   Some guarantee that no matter what happens to your job you can meet your needs by auxiliary activities which will either cut your living expenses or augment your income.

Your plan then for these eventualities will require answers now to the following questions:

1.   How secure is my job?

2.   How will I get another job if necessary?

3.   What additional skills could I acquire over the near future to cut costs and augment my income?

4.   What are my current assets?

5.   What are my current liabilities?

6.   What is my debt to asset ratio?

7.   How may I pay off my current indebtedness faster, which parts should I pay off first, which indebtedness should I refinance?

8.   Which assets represent my greatest liabilities in a time of depression?

9.   Which current expenditures can I reduce as being superfluous?

10.   What percentage of my after-tax income is devoted to debt service?

11.   In the near future do I expect a job change or a transfer to another area?

12.   Within the next 10 years do I plan to retire?

13.   What percentage of my assets may be classified as having high, low, or average liquidity?

14. How many family members will I have to support five years from now, 10 years from now?

15. If we wished to augment our food supply with a garden would that entail moving?

16. Given a future expectancy of higher prices what steps can I take to cut energy costs?

17. How can we reduce our taxes now by planning our expenditures to take advantage of legal loopholes?

18. How may we defer current income tax-free to provide later retirement income?

19. How much time will we need to reach our depression proof goals?

20. How vulnerable is my income from rents and other investments in a time of depression?

Your plan will require answers to these questions plus answers to many other questions that affect your personal financial future. For example, what are your chances that your mother will have to live in a nursing home at $2,000 to $3,000 per month, etc.?

Preparation of your plan should include an accounting approach in which every aspect of your present life style is evaluated as either a positive or negative aspect in a time of depression. Once you have conducted your analysis, item by item, and written it out on paper you will likely find that your depression proof plan cannot be accomplished overnight by simply selling some assets to pay off your existing liabilities. What you have to do is to review your entire lifestyle, your income and outgo to determine which things you should do differently in order to:

1. Cut your living expenses.

2. Reduce your indebtedness.

3. Reduce your vulnerability to a job loss or other catastrophic changes.

Changes in lifestyle can cut expenses by giving up those non-productive things you do now or cost cutting alternatives. Further you may augment your income as well by selling or bartering some of your products. You can cut your living expenses now and increase your income now, without any delay, by engaging in one or more of the following activities:

Raise rabbits, chickens, bees, goats, pigs, sheep, cattle

Raise a garden

Learn to milk

Repair your own automobile

Buy oil by the case and change your own oil

Mow your own lawn

Fix the plumbing

Hunting and fishing

Dig clams

Gather wild mushrooms, asparagus, berries

Cut firewood

Do you own carpentry

Can or freeze vegetables

Make sausage

Put in a wood stove

Make your own wine or beer

Grind wheat or cereal

Handload ammunition

Learn to bake without mixes

Buy food in quantity

Do your own electrical wiring

Roll your own cigarettes

Cure hams and bacon

Smoke fish

Repair your own TV

Build furniture

Learn to weld

Stop buying pizzas and TV dinners

I know this sounds anachronistic, a retreat to a pioneer life-style. It's what your parents or grandparents left behind when they moved from the farm to the suburbs. Even so, some of these strategies may make sense in your future. The important thing is that you learn some of these things now, before it is an absolute necessity. There are courses at your local Vo-Tech center which offer the opportunity to learn welding, carpentry, electrical wiring, plumbing, cooking, canning, and automobile repair. Even, if by chance, the depression is postponed, it will be to your advantage to know how to do those things. Meanwhile take stock of your current lifestyle to see how you spend your leisure time. Golf, tennis, bike riding, skiing, water skiing, hang gliding, and other such sports may be fun and they may be good exercise, but they don't contribute a damn thing to the family budget. In fact, they represent an expense. You can get just as good exercise cutting firewood, hunting, fishing or raising a garden, and the net result is both exercise and an economic benefit. Give it some thought and sell your golf clubs now while there is still a demand for them, for there won't be much demand in a depression. Today with automobile mechanics, plumbers and electricians charging $60 to $80 per hour for their time, why should your spare time be frittered away for nothing? Maybe you can't do as good a job as the professional tradesman but every hour you spend doing your own repairs is worth his wage plus the income tax you would have paid on that much income.

Look around you and see who are those who have already modified their lifestyle in this manner. They include the hippies and many of those now retired. They won't feel the depression, in fact many of them won't notice it, for they have their small property paid off and through their gardens and livestock they are producing their own food. Their purchases at the grocery store look like this:

Flour

Margarine and cooking oil

Sugar and coffee

Salt and tobacco

and costs about $100 a month and that's a far cry from your present monthly grocery bill, right?

The do it yourself syndrome is both a way to beat the economic trap and also a means of achieving peace of mind and a feeling of security. You know you are in control of your own welfare and you are not dependent upon the whims of your boss, company management, or the government. You know who's in charge, you are.

A good place to start is to subscribe to the *Mother Earth News* and buy a copy of the *Whole Earth Catalogue*. There is plenty of advice available in those and other how to do it books. You can even build your own house, as we did in New Mexico, as a means to cut costs. For example, if you are nearing 55 and have most of your equity tied up in your home you should give serious thought to building your retirement home now. You could then sell your present home, taking advantage of the $500,000 one-time tax exemption from capital gains and use that money to pay off all your debts. If you do all the work yourself your retirement home could cost much less, in the $20 to $30 per square foot range.

We actually built our adobe in New Mexico for $2 per square foot by scrounging most of the materials. Of course that was years ago and there is no chance of repeating those costs today. Even so you could build your second home for $20,000—$50,000 and get a lot closer to that depression proof future.

While we are on the subject of retirement homes you should give serious thought to where that home should be located. An important consideration is the cost of living and that varies by state. Especially important are the taxes assessed by the individual states.

Average of State and Local Taxes Ranked from Highest to Lowest

1. Massachusetts
2. New York
3. Minnesota
4. Wisconsin
5. Maryland
6. New Jersey
7. Michigan
8. Rhode Island
9. Connecticut
10. Oregon
11. California
12. Vermont
13. Hawaii
14. Pennsylvania
15. Kentucky
16. Colorado
17. Illinois
18. District of Columbia
19. New Hampshire
20. Alaska
21. Utah
22. Iowa
23. Maine
24. Arizona
25. Delaware
26. North Carolina
27. Virginia
28. Kansas
29. South Dakota
30. Missouri
31. Washington
32. Idaho
33. Montana
34. South Carolina
35. Indiana
36. North Dakota
37. Nebraska
38. Georgia
39. Ohio

40. Alabama
41. Arkansas
42. Mississippi
43. New Mexico
44. Nevada
45. Oklahoma
46. Florida
47. West Virginia
48. Texas
49. Tennessee
50. Wyoming
51. Louisiana

On taxes alone the ten best states to retire in include Alabama, Arkansas, Mississippi, New Mexico, Nevada, Oklahoma, Florida, West Virginia, Texas, Tennessee, Wyoming and Louisiana. If you select from that list those states in the Sun Belt where heating costs are low you can cut your living costs even more.

As an example states with the highest taxes charge two to three times as much as the lowest taxing states. If we assume that heating costs in the Sun Belt are equally lower, a move from Massachusetts, New York, Minnesota, Wisconsin, or Maryland to one of the low taxing Sun Belt states could save you $2,000-$5,000 or more per year.

Even if you are not ready for retirement the same situation exists tax wise for those in the higher income brackets. Therefore if you consider a job change you should be aware of the tax and heating advantages of the Sun Belt states.

Continuing our focus on cost cutting we recommend shopping the garage sales to cut the cost of consumable goods. Over the years our experience has been that practically anything you can think of can be purchased at garage sales at 10% to 15% of the new prices.

This subject has already been covered in greater detail in *The Penny Capitalist* (Horatio 1979) so you can add that book to your list of recommended reading. The same is true with respect to cutting your tax bill by creative exploration of the deductions available to you. *The Penny Capitalist* covers that topic as well.

The secret of a depression proof future is dependent upon a dedicated effort to cut your current living costs in every way possible. Meanwhile you should use the funds so freed to reduce your indebtedness to a more manageable level. Finally the depression proofing requires some changes in your investments so that the investments you hold are those that will either increase in value during a depression or at least preserve most of your capital.

Reducing indebtedness and shifting your assets from those that face a high vulnerability in a depression to depression proof investments does not necessarily require that you come up with cash. In fact the sale of one asset such as real estate in order to purchase another asset such as silver coins would require that you pay out part of your equity in capital gains tax since inflation has led to a gain in your present equity. Far better is to trade what you have for what you want since therein lies no tax liability. Meanwhile you have shifted the potential depression liability from yourself to another. The following ads from Coin World illustrate how such a transaction might be set up. Note that practically anything may be traded, stamps, lots, houses, Nazi collectibles, comic books etc. These ads gave names and addresses to contact. Those have been deleted here since they are not pertinent to our inquiry.

> PRIVATE PARTY desires large collection of U.S. material. Have for trade Colorado Mountain land, ranch with trout stream plus irrigated farmlands. All inquiries confidential.

> WILL TRADE for U.S. silver coins beautiful spacious two story family home over 100 years old in St. Lawrence County upstate NY. Exquisite woodwork, 4 bedrooms, 2 baths, 2 car garage, close to major resort areas in U.S. and Canada. Lake Placid only 2 hour drive. Write.

> GRAND CANYON area, AZ, Route 64. Less than 30 miles south; 8 lots worth approximately $5,000. Best trade offer.

The next step in your depression proof plan, after you have identified your assets and liabilities and have selected those auxiliary skills that you will develop, is to place your proposed actions on a specific time schedule. You will pay off your current credit cards by X date, your car by X+1, and your home by X+2. You will acquire that nest egg of silver or gold coins by X+3 and so forth. The plan is simple and two fold. You simultaneously cash in some of your inflationary gains in real estate or other investments and use those proceeds to reduce you debt exposure.

Refinancing is another way to reduce your debt exposure. Even if refinancing does not reduce your overall debt, you may be able to pay it off sooner or combine several loans into one. Another gambit is to diversify your risk. For example, do not carry all of your indebtedness in the same name. If bankruptcy were threatened which property would you want to keep and which would you be willing to lose first? Once you know which property you want most, such as your home, borrow money on other assets to pay off the home. Then form a family corporation or trust and place those assets with the greatest indebtedness in that name. Such a ploy puts you in the position of being a separate legal entity from the corporation or trust. If the latter goes bankrupt you still own your home free and clear. By such a maneuver, even if you can't reduce your indebtedness, you can at least reduce your overall risk.

Another part of your plan must be a review of all of your current investments. Those that aren't doing so well should be liquidated. However at this point in time we may ask whether or not those funds should be reinvested? Are there any reasonably secure investments? The smooth moves would thus appear to be either:

1.   Use your funds to reduce your indebtedness.

2.   Buy gold and silver coins as a hedge against further inflation and devaluation of the dollar.

3.   Put some funds into foreign stocks or bonds as a hedge against devaluation of the dollar.

4.   When interest rates fall, refinance.

For example, one of the few bargains currently available is borrowed money. Interest rates today are at a 40-year low. The question is can you repay if you borrow more and what can you buy with the borrowed funds that will protect your future? I would caution against buying income property at today's prices unless:

1)You can pay cash, or 2) you can locate a bargain property priced at least 20% below market. Purchase of income property at today's prices with an agreement to meet up to 30 years of payments seems to me to be exceedingly risky.

If you are currently considering selling your present home in order to buy a larger one, give serious thought to remodeling. Remember that even if the new home only costs $30,000 to $50,000 more, and that's probably minimal, you will be paying interest on that amount for the next 25-30 years. Is one additional room worth that plus $25,000 or so in interest? It makes more sense to add a room for $10,000-$20,000. If you do the work yourself those costs can be cut in half.

What about remodeling, is it a good investment? Probably not, if your goal is to resell. According to Money Magazine (August 2002, p. 107) remodeling your basement may increase your living space but may not be a financial winner. Nationally, remodelers who then sold recovered an average of only 69% of their remodeling costs. Some markets were higher than others but the majority recovered from 39% to 94% of their cost. Only those remodeling in San Francisco, Birmingham, and Seattle realized a profit.

Investment Strategy—A Stitch in Time

In a time of a crash and the ensuing depression your investment goals are not to make money but to avoid losing money. You must adopt a conservative stance which will permit you to retain what assets you have rather than lose them. As others all around you are losing their assets what you possess will gain in value, leaving you in better relative position than before the crash. However in order to do this you must take defensive action prior to the crash. After the crash it's too late since everyone is in the same boat and are trying to sell their speculative assets at whatever price they can get. The lesson we have learned from the history of depressions is that assets in banks are of little value because of bank failures, bank closures, and restrictions placed on withdrawals. Assets in real estate are vulnerable for both the equity owner and the mortgage lender. Rents dropped 65% between 1929 and 1932 forcing numerous foreclosures since the income did not meet the costs of the payments on the existing mortgages. The costs of ownership were similar and with a drop in per capita income foreclosures were the order of the day.

The situation is opposite to that prevailing in a time of infla-
tion. In inflation debtors are rewarded and creditors are the losers.
In a depression the winners are those with cash and paid up assets.
Harry Schultz (1972, pp. 203-222) discusses the advantages and
disadvantages of each kind of investment in a time of deflation.
His recommendations are that in a crash the investor:

Avoids	Holds
Debt	Cash
Illiquid banks	Strong foreign currencies
Small banks	A paid off home
Banks with large	Hedge funds?
international deposits	Government bonds
Savings and Loan Assoc.	AA Corporate bonds
Leaving cash with brokers	
Weak currencies	Silver
Mortgages	Gold**
Commodities	
Stocks	
Mutual funds	
Municipal bonds	
Convertible debentures	
Art	
Antiques	

The items are singled out by Schultz in his analysis on the
basis of liquidity and the guarantee of income. He views with sus-
picion any operation which places your assets under the care or
control of others. He further expresses his doubts as to the ability
of municipal bonds, convertible debentures, or real estate mortgages to continue their promised return in the face of reduced
income. Even silver as a deflation hedge is questioned by Schultz
since its primary use is industrial rather than monetary and in a
time of deflation industrial demands would be reduced.

Your strategy for investment then should be to get into a
stronger cash position, with fewer debt obligations as you perceive
the inflationary spiral to be approaching closer and closer to a
crash. Such advice is, of course, standard. The problem is in assessing when the crash is imminent. The only advice that bears

** the only sure bet!

remembering here is that it is far better to sell your speculative assets some time in advance of the crash rather than after. Too soon is infinitely better than too late!

The way to accomplish this transition from an inflationary portfolio of investments to a deflationary one is to appraise your holdings on a semi-annual or quarterly basis. As you sell some because they have become too speculative, use the proceeds to reduce your debt exposure on those you still hold. You may say it's already too late because of the collapse of the Internet companies in 2000-2002. In a sense that's true, however in all times there are those who don't get the message. Those are the ones you sell to. Further, we don't know how far down is the bottom—how far down things may yet go.

Learn to Live Off the Land

Living off the land is not difficult, it simply requires some effort and a little dedication. I remember the hippie commune who lived nearby. It was a great trauma the day they bought a goat and someone had to learn to milk it, everyone being afraid she might kick! They also lost their garden because of a conflict of values. They didn't believe in pesticides so solved the bug problem by picking bugs off the leaves. Unfortunately, the bugs multiplied faster than they could pick so eventually the bugs were declared the winners since there weren't any leaves left on the plants. Another problem was that the commune members had to wait until the "ground karma" was right before they could dig in the garden. They also had to decide which members would keep up "the spiritual end of things" and which would work in the garden. Their record wasn't too successful but yours can be better with a minimum of effort.

Several items are of importance in living off the land. Primarily you can obtain a degree of independence from the grocery store. At the same time do not assume that you can meet all of your needs off the land. Subsistence farming is just that, in exchange for full time effort you can gain a subsistence level return. What works best is to augment your present income with some food raised in a garden. A small garden can yield all the tomatoes, corn, onions, squash, green pepper, etc. that you need for the entire year. Even if you don't grow a garden you can cut costs by buying vegetables and fruits in late summer and fall and then canning or freezing them. Other activities can be viewed as a gainful hobby such as raising rabbits, bees, etc. One of the financially most rewarding activities is to keep a milk cow. You can save $2 a day or so by not buying milk. Of course you need a place to keep the cow which eliminates most subdivisions. On the negative side the cow has to be milked every day which poses a real problem since it interferes with those three-day weekends at the beach.

Hunting, fishing, clam digging, gathering mushrooms, wild asparagus, etc. are also ways to obtain food from nature. Having hunted deer and elk for a number of years I can relate that it takes a lot of skill to meet your expenses by bringing home game every year. The total costs of licenses, gas, camping equipment, rifles, ammunition, rental of horses or 4-wheel drive vehicles, etc., can make the overall cost per pound pretty high. The secret is to devote your energies to learning the habits of game animals. You don't need a $500 Browning automatic rifle if your skill at hunting puts you within 50 yards of your quarry. Care of any dead game is also very important. A typical greenhorn trick is to bring their game home on a hot day tied to a fender. When they get home the meat has spoiled.

I am not proposing that you become a modern Daniel Boone. All I suggest is that you consider whether any portion of living off the land makes sense in conjunction with your existing life-style. For example, supplementing your diet with ducks, rabbits, quail, pheasant, could also provide that weekend exercise you have been needing.

Home canning and freezing is another way to get ahead in the fight against the supermarket checkout counter. Did you know that 35% of home canners live in cities of 100,000 or more? I will not detail canning methods here. What is important is to follow proper procedures to avoid botulism. For many, freezing is the easy way to preserve food. Last year for example, I boiled tomatoes down to sauce and then put them in plastic freezer cartons. You would be amazed how many tomatoes it takes to make a gallon of spaghetti sauce. I also harvest fruit and make jelly. So far I've used plums, chokecherries, crabapples, and even prickly pear!

Another source growing on the land which has become of increasing importance lately is wood. Most kinds of trees can be used for firewood although hardwoods, such as maple, pine, pinon, fir, and juniper, are better than the softwoods like cottonwood. If you live near a national forest give their headquarters a call as they often permit the cutting of downed or beetle killed timber for firewood without charge. The Fastest Trader in the West has gone into heating with wood in a big way. Two years ago he put in a large wood heater on the ground floor of his house. This year he has added a wood range in the kitchen and is having a metal heating unit installed in his fireplace. With high costs for heating oil he figures to save his installation costs in one winter. Since we live in the country we own our own wood lot. We have mostly locust trees growing along the irrigation ditch. They initially grow like weeds and then die after reaching diameters of 4 to 6 inches. We cut the dead ones each year, which with old fence posts, have kept us well supplied with firewood. If you don't own a source of firewood and don't live near a national forest, visit nearby farms. They may have old hedgerows, fallen-down barns, fences, etc. which you can have for the labor of removing them.

If you don't own any country property now might be an excellent time to buy that small farm which could help you cut your costs of living and help you gain financial independence.

Learn an Auxiliary Skill—Have Ph.D., will Fix Plumbing

Most of us these days are the product of an educational system in which we have been trained to become specialists. Better salaries are the result of being trained as an accountant, draftsman, teacher, lawyer, or whatever. The jack-of-all-trades is now more an unsuccessful legacy from the past who is out of step with the fast moving present. Whenever we need help in our suburban homes we call the plumber, the electrician, carpenter, rug cleaner, stone mason, etc. All charge union scale which to the homeowner is analogous to spending three minutes in the ring with Mohammed Ali. You lose every time!

A better way to approach this situation is to identify several skills you can learn to do yourself. Choose those that seem most interesting, or perhaps you have always wanted to do. Then sign up at the local Vo-Tech school and take that course in wiring, welding, carpentry or whatever. For example, in our community we have a choice of vocational courses offered by the university continuing education program, the Vo-Tech center and the local Free School. A list of the courses they offer includes the following:

Creative writing
Japanese, Chinese and Indian cooking
Reporting
Family Counseling
Bronze Casting
Photography
Videotape technique
Accounting
Beer Brewing
Sausage making
Bread making
Tax avoidance
Financial planning
Studio recording
Book publishing
Quilting
Bicycle repair
Automobile maintenance
Property management
Typewriter repair
Modeling
Herbal medicine
Glassworking

Courses are not the only opportunities offered at the local Vo-Tech center. Last year they built a modern house as a class project. They then sold it at public auction and my uncle bought it. How would you like to buy a modern three bedroom house for one third its retail value?

When signing up for courses, try to select auxiliary skills that you know would be in demand in a depression, such as shoe repair rather than a skill which could easily be dispensable such as interior decorating. Also you can obtain services cheaper at the local Vo-Tech center such as car repair or hair cuts. Use their services to cut your expenses.

Not only do the vocational courses provide you the opportunity to earn money by working for others, they also provide a means of doing your own work and saving money. For example, just learning to tune up your own car can save you a couple of hundred bucks a year. At our house we have a type of communal effort. One son welds, another can fix anything, mechanical or electrical. I do some plumbing, and our other son repairs and takes care of the cars. We don't attempt to do everything. For some plumbing, electrical work, and car repairs we do call on the professionals. However what we do costs us on the average about 20% what the professional charges. Without making a crusade out of it you could probably cut your living expenses by $1,000 a year or so by doing some of your own maintenance. For example, we needed a new window in the basement. The contractor didn't even give us an estimate. Instead he said to remind him if he hadn't gotten it fixed in two to three months. We found the perfect double glass aluminum casement window with screens at a garage sale for $7.50. My son installed the window and our only other cost was for caulking. The contractor would have charged $200 or more.

Further you need to now begin equipping your workshop with the tools you will need to carry out these auxiliary activities and home repairs. Look for them at garage sales and buy now while they are still available used at cheap prices.

A partial list includes:

Chainsaw, rototiller or garden tractor
Radial arm saw
Drill press
Table saw
Belt sander
Skilsaw
Electric drill
Jigsaw or bandsaw
Lathe
Hand tools, saw, hammer, etc.
Set of automobile wrenches
Welding equipment
Garden tools
Router

Bolts, screws, nails
Pipewrenches
Pipe cutter
Pipe threader
Tap set
Post hole digger
Ax
Wheelbarrow
Drop light
Hack saw
Bench grinder
Pick and shovel

All of these cost an arm and a leg at the local hardware store. At garage sales they are affordable. For example, I went to a garage sale and bought a bench vise for $8.00. Then they threw in a box of bolts and screws for free.

All of this advice sounds Pollyannaish, after all anyone can do simple home repairs. However how often do we take the easy way out and call the repairman just so we will have the weekend free to go to the beach or play golf. I'm guilty of that kind of weakness as well. Recently we hired the plumber to move the washer and dryer from the kitchen to the basement. He charged 12 hours labor plus the materials. The total cost was $800.00 just for hooking up the washer and dryer! I could have done it myself but I was "busy" writing this book.

If you have an auxiliary skill, in addition to your profession, you not only can save money by doing your own repairs, you can also work for others to gain additional income. Further, and this is the major point, once you have gained the auxiliary skill you have become one step closer to becoming depression proof. If you lose your present job you could have that skill to fall back on to help make ends meet until you locate the next permanent position.

Cutting your Living Costs—Toad Ointment and Other Cures

Cutting your living costs involves two major activities. The first is paying less for your consumable goods. The second consists of arranging your financial affairs so that you can preserve a larger part of your salary as take home pay. The money you save and the money you would have paid in taxes, insurance, etc. can then be used to reduce your indebtedness.

The best place to save money is at local garage sales and flea markets. You may think that the advice I am giving worked fine in the past but can't be carried out today. As an example here are the results of shopping at garage sales and thrift stores by my wife and me last weekend(October 18-19, 2002).

Purchases	Cost	Value/ Replacement Cost
10K gold Masonic lodge pin	0.10	$10.00
Gallon of linseed oil	1.00	13.00
3/4 gallon urethane varnish	1.00	30.00
10 sander belts	1.50	32.00
Electric drop light	1.50	16.00
2 Navajo silver belt buckles	5.00	100.00
17 inch color TV	7.00	80.00
Portable vacuum cleaner	5.00	40.00
Pair azurite earrings	2.00	15.00
	$24.10	$336.00

My estimate of the replacement cost of the appliances is the price you would pay in a second hand appliance store. New price would be two or three times as much but that's not relevant since these were used appliances. The TV works fine, in fact it has a better picture that our other TV, which is fifteen years old. We could afford to buy a new TV but why bother as long as the one we have works. The Navajo belt buckles are the type made in the 1970's with inlaid chips of turquoise and coral. One was even marked sterling so it's hard to understand why the thrift store had them priced so cheaply. The silver content alone is worth $20.00, since they weigh two ounces each. Retail they would be priced at $100.00 each. However you can buy similar ones in the Gallup pawnshops for $40.00 to $50.00 each. If advertised on E-Bay you should be able to sell them for $50.00 each. So, you can see it still is possible to buy items of real wealth for less than they are worth. The other items, linseed oil, etc., I use in my woodworking shop. At the local hardware store such supplies are outrageously expensive. For example, I was amazed that a gallon of varnish costs up to $52.00! Our cost was about 7% of estimated value. You could perhaps cut the new price by 10% to 20% by vigorous shopping at the discount stores. Even so, by shopping the garage sales for those items we would still be at least $200.00 ahead.

We saved $300.00 in buying consumer items in one weekend. Add to that the income tax saved, $75.00, and multiply those savings, $375.00 per week, times 52 weeks and you can see that it would require a salary increase of $19,500 per year to equal our savings in purchasing power. It isn't just how much you earn that counts but also what you do with it. Of course we don't shop the garage sales every weekend, so the above estimate is exaggerated, however you get the idea.

There are lots of other ways to cut your costs. You can salvage building materials or firewood from construction sites or the city dump. Even agricultural crops are often available at discount if you do the picking. My friend, The Apartment Pyramider, told me he had even seen a sign at a farm which stated, "milk -45 cents per quart, you milk it." Other ways to save include joining a discount food co-op, buying dented cans in the grocery store, patronizing the day old bread store, and buying oversize and spot eggs. Even meat is available at discount. One way is to buy half of a beef carcass or more. However you have to know what you're buying, as there are lots of fast freezer beef salesmen who aren't selling what you think they are. Beef carcasses are sold according to yield grade as follows:

Yield grade 1	no fat
Yield grade 2	slight amount of fat
Yield grade 3	plenty fat
Yield grade 4	Lotsa fat or some lean
Yield grade 5	disgustingly fatty

Fat is worth about three cents per pound so don't buy it if you can avoid it. Carcasses are priced at so much per pound hanging weight. This figures as follows: the weight is warm carcass weight which, due to evaporation of body fluids, is several percentage points or pounds less than what you pay for. Assuming a 1,000 pound live steer, the carcass weight would be close to 600 pounds. Depending upon the yield grade there will be from 25% to 35%

trim loss due to fat. Bone makes up an additional 14% to 16%. The finished packaged product is then about 400 pounds out of the 1,000 pound steer. You pay something like $2.00 per pound times the 600 pound carcass weight or $1,200 plus 10 cents a pound cutting and wrapping charge times 600 pounds = $60.00. Your total cost is $1,260 for 400 pounds of usable product. Your true cost then is not the $2.00 per pound that was advertised. It is $3.15 per pound. The next time you shop for a beef carcass run these figures through your calculator first to see how good a deal you are getting. When buying a carcass be sure to ask what yield grade it is since that was established by the USDA inspector and you have a legal right to know that quality grade just as much as whether the carcass is also graded Prime, Choice, Good, Standard, etc. The only animals to buy are those that grade Choice and are Yield grade 1 or 2. Prime is too fatty and all other grades are from older tougher animals. High "good" grade is also Ok if the animal is less than three years of age. Never buy a yield grade 4 or 5 animal and if the processor won't tell you the yield grade don't buy any animals from him. Another practice to be wary of is buying a live animal and then having it processed. You have to be careful that the processor gives you your meat back, not meat from a 12-year-old reject. A second strategy is to buy meat from the supermarket that has been marked down for "quick sale." What my friend calls "used meat." Normally the meat is fine; it's just reached its "sell by" date. If you shop carefully, comparing prices, you can cut your costs for meat to $1.00 to $2.00 per pound. For example, a couple of weeks ago I bought two small steaks. The marked price was $3.15. The discount was $3.00, so my cost was 15 cents.

Cutting your living costs requires only two basic rules. Always look for bargains and never buy anything new or at retail price if you can avoid it. Any time you are offered something free, take it.

For example, at a garage sale we were offered a TV set that had no picture, only snow. In ten minutes at home, using only a screwdriver, my son was able to reset the horizontal hold and obtain a perfect picture. Our cost was zero.

Even if you can't use something you get for free you may be able to trade it later for something useful. If not, it's possible to give it to your favorite charity and legally be eligible for a tax deduction. Also, of course, any food you raise or gather wild cut your costs of living. If you are producing food research into organic farming has revealed that one way to cut costs is to stop using commercial fertilizers. Farmers now are finding that crop rotation and use of manure leads to greater soil fertility, less erosion, and better soil conditions. Crop yields are as high and because fertilizer costs are less, profits are greater.

The next step to free up more spending money is to look for a tax shelter. They come in many forms but include mortgage interest paid, depreciation, any business expense, the investment tax credit, and others. What is clear is that without arranging your affairs to claim as many tax deductions as legally possible you are paying too much of your salary in tax. Again the *Penny Capitalist* tells you how. Also you could consult Mooney's book (1991) on tax shelters and estate planning. The other item to arrange is that portion of your earnings that are invested before income taxes are assessed, such as IRA's, Keogh, or 203B plans. In addition, the income on the investment plan is also reinvested tax-free. Upon retirement you can cash in your account or make regular monthly withdrawals and then pay tax at what is expected (according to conventional wisdom) to be at a lower rate since your retirement income is expected to be lower. Whereas this is standard investment advice—put some of your present income into a tax sheltered retirement plan so you can pay lower taxes later—inflation threatens even this utopia. If inflation goes wild then maybe you won't be receiving investment income on your plan at a rate that exceeds the rate of inflation. Then when you draw your funds out, say 20 years from now, inflation may have pushed you into an even higher tax bracket. In short, such tax wise estate planning, if galloping inflation returns, poses risks which cannot be accurately assessed on the basis of current information. On the other hand what you do know is that if you don't put some of your funds into such a tax sheltered plan today you *will* pay tax on all of your current income.

Another bargain area consists of knowing where to borrow money. Interest rates vary and some shopping around will pay off in either a lower interest rate, a lower monthly payment, fewer points, a better collateral arrangement, or some other option advantageous to you. My advice is to shift your borrowing business regularly between several lenders. When you get ahead a little, refinance to cut down the number of loans you are carrying. If you are overextended borrow from one lender to pay off another. Even if you can't currently reduce your indebtedness you can at least maintain a good credit rating. In applying the concept of "Creative Borrowing" you don't borrow at the convenience of the lender according to their rules, you stretch their rules to meet your needs.

The main point concerning our discussion on cutting your living costs is that it must be a comprehensive program in which every portion of your budget is reviewed to determine how costs may be cut. When you put that plan into operation the money saved can then either be used to reduce your indebtedness or to make new investments.

One way to cut the high cost of living is to stop paying doctors for the exorbitant cost of medical care. Treat yourself and your family at home with home remedies such as that from the recipe that follows:

> "Toad ointment—for sprains, lame-back, rheumatism, caked breasts, caked udders, etc.

> Good size live toads, 4 in number; put into boiling water and cook very soft; then take them out and boil the water down to 1/2 pt., and add fresh churned unsalted butter 1 lb,. And simmer together; at the last add tincture of arnica 2 ozs.

> ...some persons might think it hard on toads, but you could not kill them quicker in any other way (Chase, 1867, p. 130).

Actually I'm not serious in proposing that you rely on do-it-yourself medical care and "toad ointment" points that fact out pretty well. While you can cut your costs by do-it-yourself solutions, there is a reasonable limit.

Chapter 9
How to Cope with
Runaway Inflation

Runaway inflation is that phenomenon in which everyone comes to expect inflation to continually get worse. Their expectations are reflected in price increases which are not based on increased costs of production but on an increase in the inflationary premium. Prices go up because people expect them to go up so they raise their price in advance. In effect everyone is chasing his own tail and those who stockpiled goods in advance reap major windfalls.

How to cope with runaway inflation requires that you prepare in advance by cutting costs wherever you can as we have discussed previously. Then you must have something of value put aside to sell when prices really get out of hand. One of the very best items to have for sale of course is food. If you can produce a surplus of food from your garden, bees, cattle, rabbits, etc., and have some for sale during runaway inflation you will always have buyers. The items that should be stockpiled in advance include all kinds of consumable items. Howard Ruff (1979) makes a major point that food storage, dried, preserved, and canned food, is your most important first step. He recommends that you store one year's supply in advance. Other items to buy up and store include anything with an extended shelf life, canned oil, grease, household cleaners, paper products, ammunition, liquor, wine, anything consumable that will not spoil. Ruff's point, and it is well taken, is that with high inflation anything you buy and store and then use two years from now could yield a 25% to 30% saving. The message is, in order to beat runaway inflation, buy now and consume later. Fuel oil and gasoline are also excellent buys to store, if you have a tank, since we have all experienced high prices at the pump. Our appraisal is that as long as U.S. fuel prices are less than those of Europe, the future price trend is likely to be up.

The second class of goods to store for future use in runaway inflation includes those items of real value. These include gold, silver, and diamonds. You can trade them for whatever else you might need. My recommendation is that those holdings should be in bullion coins. The coins will have a recognized value, which need not be assayed, and they can be sold with a minimal sales commission being charged. The coins can also be used outright as currency to buy whatever you need. Since in the case of totally chaotic conditions you do not know what may happen I would suggest that you keep some of your coins at home in a safe and keep the rest in a bank safety deposit box. In that case if there is bank closure you could still have access to those coins in your safe. If you are robbed at home you would still have those coins that were in the safe deposit box. Whereas holding some coins in a bank in a safe foreign country like Switzerland is the ultimate security hedge, I only believe that gambit is worthwhile if you have excess funds in the vicinity of $100,000.

In times of runaway inflation you should convert your inflationary gains by selling real estate, art, antiques, numismatic coins and other low liquidity items. Then use the proceeds to pay off your debts on the property you firmly intend to keep.

Diamonds are unique and a special hedge against unforeseen events. Whereas diamonds are a bad investment, since you cannot easily buy them wholesale, and the markup is often 100%, they are an excellent hedge. Their price is maintained by a cartel so that their value seems to never go down. Even though you have to sell at wholesale, they can give you that ultimate nest egg for financial survival. Diamonds have been the ultimate hedge for refugees throughout history.

The biggest problem in runaway inflation, other than being able to afford daily necessities, is the need to protect your capital from erosion. The following section on the Argentinean situation illustrates how such can occur.

The Argentinean Solution

Inflation in Argentina was more that 400%, and increasing at rates up to 400% per year. This was a classic case of hyperinflation and it bears study as to the day-to-day problems inflation poses and the solutions developed to cope with such a high rate of inflation. When hyperinflation was a fact of life the average Argentinean adapted his daily behavior to cope in a remarkable number of ways. A list of these solutions include:

1.   Never pass a bank without checking the interest rate offered that day.

2.   Never pass a moneychanger without checking the current currency exchange rates.

3.   Keep all your funds in a 30-day certificate of deposit.

4.   Move your funds to another bank if they pay a higher interest rate.

5.   Borrow foreign funds, then change to local currency, invest for maximum return, then convert back to foreign funds and pay off the loan.

6.   Wages and salaries are indexed to prevent inflation caused losses in buying power.

7.   Tax laws prevent inflationary gains in salaries or inventory sales from being taxed.

8.   At any time that interest rates do not keep up with inflation consumers buy up consumer items or real estate.

9.   Shop owners don't care if goods sell or not since they will be worth more in the future.

10.   Unemployment is low but workers have to be bribed with a variety of fringe benefits and payments.

11.   Job turnover is very high as workers seek the best wages.

12.   The high fringe benefits paid to permanent salaried employees makes temporary employees attractive. Therefore a high percentage of the work force are temporaries.

13.   Owing to the tremendous inflationary potential trading volume in the stock market is very high.

14.   Pensions are also indexed to prevent loss of buying power.

What all this meant in terms of the lifestyle of the average Argentinean was that all his actions were tuned to daily fluctuations in the inflation rate. He had to be constantly on guard that his investments and source of livelihood were being maximized because any other result left him a net loser. He had to be financially sophisticated and constantly on his guard. In addition, the inflationary climate turned the entire nation into speculators instead of producers. Goods were to be hoarded for higher prices rather than sold and real estate fulfilled the same function.

The lessons are here for us to observe and they are not all negative. Whereas the fact of hyperinflation in Argentina cannot be ignored, and therefore it was the central fact in their daily lifestyle, its harmful aspects were somewhat minimized. The corrective measures included indexation which prevented loss of buying power of salaries and pensions. There was a clear recognition of the distinction between inflationary gain and real gains. This distinction was codified in the tax laws to prevent losses in capital or income resulting from inflationary gains in inventory or salaries. Given widespread knowledge within the public that such distinctions existed, most Argentineans seemed to be able to cope with the system.

The negative aspects were present also. The situation consisted of a very fast paced national game of musical chairs and everyone not on his toes was a loser. In addition, the emphasis on hoarding versus production created long-term negative results.

If we may believe that the Argentineans have learned to live with hyperinflation, their solution requires almost superhuman daily dedication. Surely this is a very high price to pay in order to simply make ends meet.

A postscript—as of November 15, 2002, the Argentineans have again defaulted on $750 million worth of debt.

CHAPTER 10
HOW TO ACQUIRE REAL WEALTH

Counselors in investments normally fail to inform the would be investor the odds against his acquiring any appreciable wealth. Further our neophyte investor, who is likely to be at least middle aged or even older, is never informed as to the distinction between currency dependent assets and real wealth. As we have noted earlier real wealth is limited to tangible assets especially gold, silver, and diamonds. Whereas other assets, land, real estate, art, and antiques constitute real wealth, they are less liquid and therefore more difficult to sell. In addition their sale entails the payment of a substantial broker's commission ranging from 10% to 50% of their retail value. Diamonds are subject to this limitation as well. Only gold and silver may be sold any day of the week at prices that net the seller close to their market value. Stocks and bonds also may be sold daily with minimal commissions charged. In a depression stock prices are depressed and bonds may be defaulted. Therefore since our goal is to acquire assets now which may serve a protection against a depression we return to gold and silver as our primary investment medium. Whereas platinum is also a rare metal it has not been widely used and is therefore not easily obtainable.

Typical investments are those things which are offered at today's market price with a sales commission attached. They are promoted as yielding a profit only if the market price increases. In many cases the proposed investment is fully valued and the market does not rise but instead goes down. In such a situation the investor ends up saddled with a loss. Even if the price remains the same or goes up slightly the investor may still have a loss owing to the sales commission and the income or capital gains taxes assessed. Our conclusion is that owing to the nature of the market and our current tax structure, it is difficult for the average investor to be successful. In addition there are a number of techniques of investing that must be mastered and the average individual's personality interferes with their practice.

The average individual cannot invest successfully because:

1.   He lacks the dedication to continually acquire and evaluate information.

2.   He must project future trends on the basis of current and past information.

3.   He must employ a shifting standard against which he evaluates all information obtained. Terms such as safety, yield, and risk change in meaning as conditions change.

4.   He lacks perseverance to pursue a course of action over the long term.

5.   He lacks the courage to take a position counter to a trend.

6.   He must act on the prospect of future events rather than on past performance.

7.   He is misinformed by the investment fraternity as to his potential profits and risks.

8.   He is dealing with secondhand and selected information.

9.   He either opts for security or gambles, as he cannot comprehend the difference between taking a calculated risk and gambling.

10.   He does not question what he reads or is told.

11.   He lets others make up his mind for him.

12.   He procrastinates and neither buys or sells soon enough.

13.   He maintains a folk wisdom that structures his thinking i.e. savings accounts are safe investments, banks are safe, etc.

14.   He postpones thinking about the future.

Now that we have gotten all of that bad news about ourselves out of the way we can move forward to examine investing in today's' economic environment.

Our first recommendation is that in order to become depression proof we must avoid currency dependent investments. The reason for this is that our currency no longer functions as a repository of wealth. The value of the currency fluctuates and in inflationary times it loses value. We need our investments to be those that in inflationary times increase in value and then when the depression comes may be easily exchanged for those items we need: food, housing etc. Standard investment media do not have these attributes. Stocks, bonds, options, warrants, commodity futures, interest-bearing securities, mortgages, etc. all possess two fatal flaws: 1) They may go down in deflationary times, and 2) they are only exchangeable for currency. This situation means that not only is it difficult to invest successfully owing to limitations within one's own personality, but in addition you must choose your investment medium with care in order to avoid the possibility of cashing in a successful investment only to receive worthless currency in exchange. Such an analysis leads us to our second recommendation. The places to acquire real wealth do not include your stock brokerage firm, your friendly local bank, or any of those gentlemen who call you up on the phone offering London options, time sharing on a condominium in Vail, or other such ventures. Even your commodities broker may not be suitable since he is selling futures contracts which are merely pieces of paper with certain promises written on them. When the crash comes you will need not promises but tangible assets which, 1) are in your possession, 2) have a recognized value, and 3) may be easily exchanged for whatever you need. This fact means that the places where you can obtain real wealth include you local coin shop, jewelry store, antique shop, flea market, and the Salvation Army store. Sounds crazy doesn't it. You can't obtain real wealth at your bank, even though it is a member of the Federal Reserve System, however at your local thrift store you can. The kinds of wealth are listed below in their order of desirability. In this case desirability means that you can physically take possession of the objects and later when you wish to sell them they can be sold easily with a limited commission.

Example of Real Wealth

In order of preference	Comment
1. Gold bullion coins	Your best bet. They can be sold easily at a discount of about 6%. However they are never available at a price much below market.
2. Silver bullion coins	They can be sold easily but the discount averages 20%.
3. All items marked Sterling	They can be easily sold at a discount of 30% of the spot price. If you can wait sterling items can be sold at retail on consignments with a commission of 20% to 40%.
4. Gold scrap—jewelry, dental gold, eyeglass frames etc.	Easily sold at 70% of the spot price.
5. Numismatic coins	The dealers' buying range is 50% to 60% of retail which enables them to resell at 80% to 100% of retail. The higher the degree of rarity the higher the percentage of retail value that can be obtained. Good collections can be sold at auction with a 20% commission. Items not truly rare, such as most uncirculated U.S. silver dollars, will sell at bullion coin prices during a major depression. Even rare coins may take considerable time to sell

at more than 50% of their value. Grading of coins is very important in establishing price and all buyers grade very conservatively. Conversely when they sell they grade very liberally. A further problem with numismatic coins is that they sell at several hundred to several thousand percent of their bullion value; therefore a substantial downside risk is present.

6. Silver scrap

Easily sold at 70% of the spot price; however if the silver percentage is in doubt the price will be lower or the buyer may refuse to buy.

7. Gold and silver jewelry

Jewelry is normally sold at two to four times its melt value. When you resell you may have to sell at the bullion price discounted 30%.

8. Diamonds and other gemstones

Can always be sold, but the typical buyer is a dealer who will offer 25% to 50% of retail. Diamonds pose a further problem in that major price differences are based on minute quality differences only visible under magnification. Such distinctions are not easily discernable by the average investor.

9. Antiques

The quality is easily discernible by a knowledgeable buyer. The seller must also know that value or he may be taken by an unscrupulous buyer. A fair price is 50% to 80% of retail. Consignment commissions range from 20% to 40%. Consigned items may take forever to sell. Items in quantity should probably be sold at auction, where the commissions average 20%. Unless you can sell enough items to make up a sale which can be individually advertised—sale at auction could lead to low prices.

10.	Guns	Collector guns are a good hedge against inflation. Normally their resale is to a dealer at 50% to 60% of market value.
11.	Art	The fine art market is a relatively thin market at all times. During a depression prices will definitely be depressed. Sale at auction normally returns the most to the seller.
12.	Real estate, land, stocks and other equities	All illiquid assets such as these should be purchased during a depression, not sold.

Gambits for Acquiring Real Wealth

Having enumerated the major categories of real wealth in their order of preference based on retention of value and ease of disposal, we may now identify ways for you to acquire a nest egg of real wealth.

The first place to start is right in your own home. You should make a consistent search through all your possessions to locate any heirlooms or other assets that you have forgotten about. Your grandmother's wedding ring that doesn't fit you may well have $100.00 worth of gold in it. The coin collection you made when you were a kid, of coins saved out of circulation could be worth a lot more than you think. The Kennedy halves that your aunt gave to the kids are now valuable—not because they are rare but because they contain 40% silver.

Other Gambits for Acquiring Real Wealth

Another way to add to your wealth is to become a buyer of gold and silver. In that way you can name the price you are willing to pay somewhere below the current market price. Typical buyers pay 50% to 70% of spot while refiners pay more—up to 80% or even 90%. Therefore you can resell what you don't choose to keep at a substantial profit. All that you need is an accurate scale, some acid for testing, a hand calculator, and a small bankroll of cash. You need not be nervous about buying since any item you are uncertain of can be rejected. Beware of gold jewelry with letters in addition to the carat mark. Normally this means that the item is gold-filled or plated. For example H.G.E. stands for heavy gold enamel which means plated. If you don't know what the letters mean, it's best to pass that item by.

Another technique is to become a coin dealer. You can begin in a small way buying and trading coins. The next step is to attend coin shows, antique shows, or gun shows where a typical weekend booth costs $30.00. Such a location provides you the opportunity to both buy and sell. The typical wholesale price you pay is 60% of retail with the option of resale at a 20% to 40% markup. As you turn coins at a profit you simply keep part as your profit after you have sold enough to get your original investment back. When buying you have the option of buying at the bullion price. When priced for resale these coins can be priced according to their numismatic value. This was the gambit utilized by coin dealers during the 1970's. They purchased bags of U.S. silver dollars at a slight markup over the bullion value and then repriced them individually as numismatic gems. Their profit margins were often 300%. This gambit will be profitable again if we have a return to runaway inflation.

A third way to increase your nest egg is to shop the antique stores and flea market looking for items of gold, silver and jewelry with quality gemstones. You should assume when engaged in shopping that, 1) most dealers know the value of what they have, and 2) most items they have for sale are priced above their true value. Now that we have covered that bad news, the good news is that occasionally they are wrong and they let go of a sleeper at a bargain price. As an example, the Antique Lady purchased a silver teapot in an antique shop for $15.00. It was not marked sterling but did have a four-digit number on the base. It tested for silver at the silver buyer's and he paid over $600.00 for it. The moral of this little story is that at today's prices you don't have to make many such finds in order to build up a nest egg of real wealth. On the other hand a piece of silver plate is no bargain at a cheap price. The silver layer is so thin it isn't worth the cost of recovery. You must also be careful in buying gold objects in antique shops, pawn shops, etc. The average person thinks gold is incredibly valuable. Therefore the average gold ring in a pawnshop is usually priced at two to three times its bullion value. If the object is gold-filled it may be priced 10 to 20 times its true value. Typical gold-filled objects are 1/10th 10K. Since 10K is 42% gold the gold-filled object has only 4% gold content. Learn your gold identifying marks and carry a magnifying glass to read them. Learn to guess the weight of common items, rings, watch cases, etc., and when you find a ring with $100.00 worth of gold in it priced at $30.00 then buy. Perhaps your best opportunities lie in the dealers' box of scrap since that damaged ring has just as much gold in it as a perfect specimen.

While covering the antique market we must clarify the truth about weighted sterling. Weighted pieces most often are candlesticks. While they appear to have a lot of silver in them they do not. The average candle stick five inches in height contains about 3/4th of an ounce of silver. At today's scrap prices that's about $3.00. Pieces that are larger pose an even more difficult problem. The average dealer believes they may have five to ten ounces of silver in them and prices the piece accordingly. In fact the silver content may only be two to three ounces. If you are in doubt as to the amount of silver in a weighted piece it is best not to buy since once you have torn apart a weighted candlestick you can only sell it for scrap. You have destroyed any value it might have had as an antique.

Another item often available at flea markets, antique shops, etc., are small silver pins. Even if marked Sterling they may still be priced less than their bullion value. So learn to estimate weight and buy when priced at a bargain.

The best current source of real wealth at a bargain price are the local garage sales held every weekend. It is still possible to find objects of gold and silver at prices that range from 5% to 20% of their true value. Such bargains are possible because the sellers 1) do not realize that the items are valuable, 2) they know they are valuable but misjudge their weight, or 3) they do not know current bullion values.

A final source of real wealth is your local thrift store, Salvation Army, Goodwill, D.A.V., St. Vincent de Paul, and the local church charities. Such stores possess mostly clothing and worthless objects of plastic. However they occasionally have objects of gold and silver at bargain prices. Usually such items are in their jewelry section among the costume jewelry. In addition you can buy eyeglass frames. These are 1/10 12K gold-filled frames. They typically cost 50 cents to $1.00 per pair, and have $3.00 to $5.00 worth of gold in them. Since these glasses represent an accumulation over time it is usually a one shot deal but you might as well clean out their eyeglass box as well as someone else.

We have covered most of the bargain basement ways to build up your real wealth. Most of these require little capital but take up a lot of time looking. If you have a substantial sum to convert to real wealth then such penny ante methods are clearly not for you. If you have several thousand dollars to invest at one time you might advertise in your local paper that you wish to buy silver coins.

You may also be able to buy quality gemstones. I feel that the best opportunities are not in diamonds since their price is controlled by the DeBeers cartel. Other stones, sapphires, rubies, emeralds, opals, topaz, tourmalines, amethyst, and aquamarines probably possess a greater potential for price appreciation. You can consider the purchase of loose cut gemstones if you have any trips scheduled to Brazil, India, Ceylon, Southeast Asia, or Australia. However read up on the market and the quality of stones before your trip, not after. Beware of synthetic gems. They look nice but their value is $3-$5 per carat. Another problem is that the best way to sell gemstones is after they have been set in jewelry. Therefore to cash in on your investment you may have to go into the jewelry business.

An additional source of wealth consists of any natural resource on land that you own. Firewood is an example as are any bearing fruit trees, nut trees, Christmas trees, building stone etc. In our inflationary economy any such natural resources may be valuable, either as a means of reducing your living expenses or as a source of additional income. A woodlot, for example, is much more valuable now than it was several years ago. With firewood selling at up to $200.00 per cord a woodlot can cut your annual heating bill by hundreds of dollars. Recently I was thumbing through an exotic woods catalogue for cabinetmakers and learned that 3/4 inch walnut boards were priced at $5.50 per square foot. If you do not now own any land with trees you might give some thought to such a purchase since any such resources are bound to increase in value over time. You could also purchase land with known mineral wealth. Currently of course, any oil-bearing lands would be highly desirable although certainly not cheap. Mining claims with gold and silver ore are another bet as in many areas the mining industry is only now being awakened from its half-century-long slumber.

In summary, gold is where you find it, even at the Salvation Army store. A consistent search for objects of real wealth over a period of time will pay off. Bear in mind the value increase in finding something of real wealth at a bargain price can be many times the return you could get on funds loaned out at interest. For example, the Antique Lady's teapot which produced a $600.00 profit, was equivalent to the interest, at today's rates, on a savings account of $30,000 invested for a full year! Stashed away in your safe deposit box until needed, a similar find could provide your family food during a depression. In addition you should consider buying productive property which will provide those natural resources that may be expected to be in short supply in the future.

Another question is how much real wealth will you need to see you through the bad times ahead. Some writers have recommended a $1,000 face value bag of silver coins for each member of the family. Given possible future price increases even that amount could go a long way toward establishing your future financial security.

CHAPTER 11
PLANNING YOUR FINANCIAL FUTURE

In these perilous times which financial actions are the proper ones to take is a perplexing question indeed. Recently I had long talk with The Apartment Pyramider who said he was stashing his funds in Treasury Bills and waiting for the day when money would be tight and new apartments would be dumped on the market by contractors who couldn't find a buyer and at the same time couldn't afford to continue payments on their construction loans. It is a cat and mouse game and it's one The Apartment Pyramider is good at.

Meanwhile the Cattle Baron is expecting a lump sum final payment from his farm sale of several years ago. He asked me whether he should pay off his cattle loan, pay down on his loan on his business building, or buy another small farm. He further stated that his banker was reluctant to extend his cattle loan, preferring instead that he reduce the outstanding balance, which the Cattle Baron didn't want to do. I suggested he take the lump sum payment, put it into Treasury Bills and wait six months to see what bargains might appear on the market.

These are examples of the kind of investment decisions that are being made every day. Who is right or who is wrong in those decisions cannot be determined until some time in the future, after the fact. One thing is certain is that if the banks clamp down on credit, that will play a major role in creating difficulties for those borrowed to the hilt. The same action will create buying opportunities for those sitting on a nest egg of cash.

At the same time that these cause and effect relationships are taking place at the local level the stability of the dollar, interest rates, and the money supply are all being affected nationally and internationally by political decisions. Can we obtain any guidance in advance concerning potential changes in this sphere? Paul A. Volcker, former Chairman of the Federal Reserve Board, wrote an article "The Political Economy of the Dollar" (Volker, 1979). We will attempt to isolate clues helpful to your future financial decisions from his writing.

1.   The floating exchange rate system will continue to be in effect.

2.   The present system for international currency control is not stable

3.   The current system has not and cannot satisfactorily solve the balance of payments problem.

4.   The U.S. politicians are not sufficiently sensitive to international currency problems to take action prior to a currency crisis.

5.   Since no one officially mentioned devaluation of the dollar prior to devaluation of the dollar, the same will be true with respect to the adoption of a new gold-backed currency.

These conclusions mean that we can look forward to continuing instability of the dollar with its value adversely affected by the high cost of imported oil. Prior to any official action to cope with the problems we may have a complete monetary collapse. These conclusions, based on our knowledge of prior historical events such as the French Connection and the runaway inflation of 1923, confirm our belief that the best investment plan for the future should involve the accumulation of assets in real wealth. The borrowing of money to acquire such assets is also a reasonable approach during a time of inflation. The repayment of that debt could be rather painless since you would be using devalued dollars. However, given the choice between paying off current debts or buying new real estate or income property with a low down payment, the choice seems not so clear. There is a high risk currently associated with real estate owing to high prices, coupled with high vacancy rates, which lead to a negative cash flow. Rent control is another negative possibility. These considerations lead us to the recommendation of a cautious wait-and-see approach. Now seems to be a better time to either pay off debt or build up one's assets rather than to take on new long-term debt. If the current recession leads to cheaper interest rates and lower prices then could be the time to buy real estate.

Now is clearly the time to reassess your debt load and if possible decrease it. If that is not possible then the next best action plan is to not take on any new debt. Consider what you can afford and do not go into debt to:

1. Take a vacation

2. Buy a recreation vehicle

3. Buy a new car

4. Pay for college expenses

5. Buy anything you don't absolutely need

College expenses are in a different category from other indebtedness, since the student can obtain a low interest loan from the government. After graduation payments begin. No parent should add to their current indebtedness for college expenses.

Another major concern is to review your retirement plans since the future holds the possibility of both runaway inflation and a depression. Your retirement plans should include at the minimum:

1. Sale or payoff of all mortgaged property.

2. Purchase of a retirement home which offers the opportunity to grow your own food.

3. Selection of a retirement home in one of the warm, low-taxing Sunbelt states.

4.   Some alternative investments, preferably in gold or silver, which will provide a hedge against difficult times. Such investments should also be considered as providing part of your retirement income needs since, owing to hyperinflation, pension plans and social security may have reduced buying power.

5.   Do not count on rental property income to support you since in a depression rents may be minimal.

This advice is not cast in concrete since I don't know for sure what is going to happen any more than anyone else. What is important for you is to review your current situation to determine which options are open to you and then arrange your plans accordingly. When the future is here those who have made plans and carried them out will be better prepared to meet it. The only way to depression proof your future is to take action now.

What You can Expect in the Near Future

Morgan Stanley in their newsletter, *Perspectives* dated October 2, 2002, predict the following:

"Looking at data back to the 1920's, investors buying the market at P/Es broadly consistent with those of today saw returns in the 6% to 8% range over the subsequent five years."

What this means for your 401K is as follows: given market declines of 30% for the DOW and 43% for the NASDAQ in 2002, it will take five years just to recoup the losses of 2002. Earlier losses, such as those in 2001 and 2000, especially the NASDAQ, will take even longer to recoup. Therefore if you are aged 50 today, you may not see that much improvement in your retirement account before age 60. Chances are your plans for an early retirement will have to be put on hold.

Other warning signs are also on the horizon. In the book, *The Judas Economy* the authors (Wolman and Colamosca, 1997) of *Business Week* magazine, state that the post Berlin Wall economy features the triumph of capital over labor. What that means is that capital will go anywhere in the world to acquire cheap labor. Further they cite the fact that the production gains in the 1990's enriched the giant corporations at the same time as their workers lost buying power due to low wage increases coupled with continuing inflation. They state: "worker morale and productivity are suffering while bankruptcies and debts are at record highs...." They published these observations in 1997 and if anything the situation is even worse today. In any event I wouldn't place my welfare in the hands of those protesting the World Trade Organization. You have to take action on your own behalf.

The catch phase is reengineering and the result is corporate downsizing. According to a Harris poll conducted in 1996 the question was, "do you think the American dream of equal opportunity, personal freedom, and social mobility has become easier or harder to achieve in the past 10 years?" Sixty-seven percent answered that it had become harder. Today, after massive layoffs, I'm sure that even more American workers would say that achieving those goals has become more difficult, or even impossible.

The Wall Street Journal, October 10, 2002, reports on the recent market decline. The market fell to its lowest close in five years, down almost 3% for the day. The bear market is now the worst since the 1930's. The DOW is down 38% from its all-time high. The Standard and Poor's 500 is down 49%, and the NASDAQ is down 78% from its record close. Further the utilities declined 9.6%, a single day record exceeded only by the crash of 1987 and on three days in 1929. A final coffin nail, the Treasury Ten Year Note now yields only 3.57%. Where will it all end? It will end with a climactic sell off after investors give up hope for a market recovery. Then, as earnings improve, and only then, will the recovery begin. The bell weather for the eventual recovery will be when and only when the newspaper headline reads, "IBM or AT&T to hire 5,000 new workers."

Another thing you can expect are real estate vacancies. Retail and office space as well as residence rentals will have high vacancy rates. This provides an opportunity for the consumer who can bargain for cheaper rent.

What if it's already too late for you to plan for the depression? You've already lost your high paying high tech job and there aren't any others out there. *Time Magazine,* October 4, 2002, reports that 48% of those looking for jobs are highly-trained professionals and white-collar workers. When they apply for an opening they find numerous others who are better trained and have more experience applying for the same job. What can you do? The answer is to bite the bullet and recognize that your life will never be the same again. Instead of wasting your time answering ads and sending out resumes you can take other actions as follows:

1.   If you still have severance pay or a working spouse now is the time to refinance your mortgage. Refinance before your income drops. The several hundred dollars a month in interest savings will make your burden a lot lighter. Why not go with an ARM—adjustable rate mortgage. The interest rate is the cheapest available and will remain at that level for five years. Five years from now things may be better and you can refinance again.

2.   Is there any chance you can join an already existing family business operated by your brother, uncle etc.? After all think of the situation in reverse; if you apply for a job elsewhere they probably have other family members who are also out of work. Who do you think they are more likely to hire?

3.   A more drastic step is sell your home and move into something you can afford. Or, rent your house and move. Either way you reduce your monthly payments and perhaps free up some equity to:

4.   Start your own business. Open a bed and breakfast, coin laundry, butcher shop, whatever, as long as you provide necessities, not boutique items like candles or tie-dyed fabrics.

5.   Cut your living expenses by employing some of the Personal Strategies discussed below.

Personal Strategies

These strategies are suggested as means to simultaneously, meet your current living expenses, be able to give some to charity, and to accumulate real wealth during a time of high inflation and high taxes. It is a daunting task. However we do not mean to suggest that you become either a scrooge or a miser. These are suggestions as to how you may make ends meet while attaining the other goals specified above.

There are lots of personal strategies you may employ to cut

your living costs. One that is available to everyone is purchasing discount foods at your local supermarket. Some regularly stock dented cans and discounted/discontinued items in separate bins. The way to shop these bins is to buy whatever you know you will use sooner or later. Don't look for what you need today but those that you can use later. Over time stockpiling food this way gives you a supply at home to choose from. For example, you don't need pumpkin often for a pie but several times a year, at holidays, that's just what you need. You must be careful not to buy cans that are so badly damaged that they may leak. Recently I bought a number of cans of evaporated milk. A nearby can had leaked and all of them had stuck to the packing box they came in. There was nothing wrong with them, even though they had bits of cardboard stuck to the bottom. Their cost, one half of retail.

The supermarkets routinely mark down packages of meat, $1 to $4 off. The reason is that they are near their sell-by date. Normally the meat is just fine. We take it home and freeze it immediately for later use. Sometimes the discount is almost as much as the full price. Remember, every dollar saved can be spent somewhere else.

You may save by buying gasoline at discount. Some stations sell at a cheaper price than others. Since gasoline is pretty much a standard product, all the savings are yours to keep. Where we live, in Boulder, Colorado, all of the gas stations charge too much. Gas is cheaper in all of the nearby towns. Therefore whenever we go to another town we fill up. We can't go there just to buy gas as we'll use up a gallon to get there and back. However if we have a reason to go there anyway, such as a doctor's appointment, we fill up. The savings range from 10 cents to 25 cents per gallon. Since we drive two cars the potential savings are $4.00 to $5.00 per week or $200.00 per year. It's worth doing.

We receive from one to three solicitations per week for new credit cards. They all offer an interest free period if you transfer a credit balance to that new account. Theoretically you could keep switching credit cards and never have to pay any interest on your loan balance. I haven't done this so can't verify how well it might work. The reason I don't is that our Visa card account is managed by the Credit Union where my income is electronically deposited. Therefore when on a trip we can make a payment on that credit card by a transfer from our checking account at the same institution, either by phone or email. I'm willing to forgo the non-interest promise of other card issuers in order to have the convenience of all my banking transactions handled by the same institution.

Continuing our review of money-saving strategies. I do wood working as a hobby making gifts for other family members; everything from cup racks to bookshelves, picnic tables, and blanket chests. Furniture wood is expensive, average grade walnut, cherry or maple sells for $3.00 to $5.00 per board foot. I obtain my lumber free from the dumpster at the local furniture manufacturing plant. Over the last couple of years I have salvaged about $3,000 worth, which I store in a woodshed for future use. My woodworking is a hobby, however you could do woodworking fulltime with a wood supply like that. The factory uses about 50,000 board feet per month of which 10% to 20% is discarded as waste. Other sources of usable scrap lumber include the city-operated recycle facility and the annual city cleanup. For the latter, people put their discards at the curb for pickup. It's free and every 2 x 4 you pick up is worth at least a dollar.

My brother-in-law has built his own band saw mill. He can cut logs up to 20" in diameter and 20' long. He lives in the woods in Washington state and salvages logs left over from commercial timber cutting. He uses the free lumber for his own construction projects. He also cuts logs for others and could earn a living that way if he wished to. You might not want to build your own sawmill but they are commercially available at prices beginning at about $6,000. When a single dead walnut tree can have $1,000 worth of lumber in it having your own sawmill could pay off.

Another money saving strategy consists of checking the dumpsters that line the alley behind your house. Dumpster Diving is not practiced much by the middle class. However it can yield perfectly usable items at a price you can afford, namely free. I spent a day a couple of years ago patrolling the alley in Denver accompanied by a professional Dumpster Diver who makes his living by salvaging items which he later resells. He knows exactly what is salable and what isn't. He takes the salable items to various second hand stores and exchanges them for cash. Typical items discarded by your neighbors include furniture, lamps, kitchen appliances, kitchen utensils, telephones and other electronics, plus books, magazines and clothing. What is interesting is if the item is in good condition it may not be thrown into the dumpster but placed in boxes next to the dumpster for ready pickup. Al the Diver told me his best find was an antique Tiffany lamp which he sold for $10,000. I can't verify his story but it's plausible as such a lamp would be worth at least $20,000.

Other salvageable items include scrap metal. Computer parts often have gold plated circuits. If you locate a quantity of these then there are recyclers who will buy them. Copper and brass scrap brings close to a dollar a pound. Electrical wiring and plumbing parts are easily sold to a metal buyer. Aluminum is also recycled, pots, pans, wiring, and cans. At 20 cents per pound salvaging aluminum cans is a penny ante deal unless you have a high volume source such as a bar or an apartment building. The Apartment Pyramider collected cans from the dumpster adjacent to a 60 unit apartment house. The renters began saving the cans for him. What they didn't know was that he owned the building.

When dumpster diving it's best to be careful. There may be discarded needles, dog waste, and other things too fierce to mention. What works best is some kind of grabber like those scissor tongs used in fireplaces. They permit you to reach to the bottom of the dumpster while avoiding anything nasty or dangerous.

Another place to check are the dumpsters behind the office complexes. Those businesses routinely discard office furniture and office supplies such as notebooks, paper, blank CDs, recording tape, etc. Where engaged in manufacture their discards include coaxial cable, electronic parts and computers. If it's something you can use it beats buying it in a store. A couple of years ago I salvaged an antique oak desk that was discarded behind one of those complexes. In an antique store it would be priced for sale for several hundred paper dollars.

Salvage opportunities are wherever you find them. My son repairs Hammond organs. Recently he dismantled one for parts and gave me the oak cabinet. Slightly remodeled it's now my computer desk.

As bankruptcies increase and as workers are laid off or reduced to part-time they will begin to reduce their expenditures.

They will have to. One way to cut costs is to drop your cable TV service, cell phone, and computer server. Other high cost non-essentials include skiing, golf, restaurant meals, and coffee at Starbucks.

Most states have a liberal tax policy that permits the owner to fall behind in property tax payments for several years before foreclosure is initiated. When that happens the taxing authority normally sells tax liens. Investors buy the tax liens at auction which means they pay the back taxes and fees. If later the owner redeems the back taxes then the investor gets his money back plus liberal interest, up to 14% in some cases. Otherwise, after a legally specified interval ... in Colorado it's three years... you may apply for a deed to the property. The taxes are a fraction of the value of the property, so heads you win, tails you win. You either get your money back plus liberal interest or you get the property. It's a win-win deal.

Another strategy consists of barter. In the depression of the 1930's it was commonplace to pay your doctor by giving him a chicken or some other item off the farm. Today, in the service economy, it is more likely that barter will take the form of exchange of services. I'll fix your car and you will provide your professional services, legal, accounting, or whatever.

Try the bargain stores, they offer standard merchandise at discount prices. We shop at one in Colorado Springs which specializes in discounted groceries, household items, and pharmaceuticals. Recently we bought long life light bulbs. They retail for $14.00 each but are supposed to last for eight years and to save $8.00 per year in electricity. We paid $1.00 per bulb. Installed the eight bulbs we are using will save us $64.00 per year, an 800% return. If they actually last eight years, the total return would be $512.00 or 6,400% on our original investment.

You can sell items on E-bay auctions. Buy things of value at garage sales and then advertise on the Internet. A friend does this and has now sold more than 1,000 items on the net.

You should raise some of your own food. For example, my sister-in-law just sent us an email:

It's finally fall here and it's so nice after a hot summer. We got the honey from the bees last week. Twenty-three pounds of honey from the super on top of the hive. The garden did pretty well too, and we've given our friends veggies and plums from the orchard, which were really nice this year.

I haven't discussed the single greatest expense the average consumer faces in his or her lifetime. Owning and operating an automobile is an incredible drain on the average family budget. You can't truly afford one and you can't live and work in America without one. It is an insoluable dilemma. Various studies on the costs, depreciation, interest, and maintenance indicate that the total costs of owning and operating vehicles over 50 years of a driving lifetime exceed $200,000 (Glickman 1981). That estimate is based on driving 15,000 miles per year, buying cars new and driving them twelve years each, which would incur 100% depreciation. The costs average $4,600 per year. Only compacts are cheaper, $3,300 per year. If you took the savings in owning a compact, $1,313 per year, and invested those savings each year at 8% (a rate that's currently unobtainable) for the 50-year term, the principal and interest would total $814,174(Glickman 1999, p. 173). However those kinds of savings are something to think about. However these figures aren't the whole story as we Americans own an average of 1.5 cars per household nationwide so we're paying out $6,900 per year for wheels.

So how can you reduce your automobile costs? Comparative studies of costs suggest it really is cheaper in the long run to buy a four-year old car and run it until the wheels fall off. In the book "The Millionaire Next Door" (Stanley and Danko 1996) the authors reveal that the average "millionaire" in their study drove an eight-year-old Buick! By buying used and avoiding the first four high depreciation years this strategy can save 25% to %30 of the new purchase price. Are those savings eaten up by increased maintenance costs? I don't really think so as automobile repair bills seem to me to be outrageous no matter whether the car is two years old or ten.

We own two cars that represent the advantages of buying used. In 1986 I bought a 1969 Pontiac Tempest for $400.00. I've driven it 4,000 to 5,000 miles per year for fifteen years commuting to my office. Annual maintenance has been about $200.00, and depreciation has averaged $27.00 per year. The bad news is that with its 350 engine it's a gas hog. As they say I get 24 miles per gallon, 14 on the highway and 10 in town, so my operating costs are increased by having to buy an extra tank of gas each month, about $200.00 per year.

Our second car is a 1987 Mercedes 300E. We bought it in 1992 when it had 28,000 miles on it. I suspect it had been a lease car. Our purchase price was 50% of its original new price. We've driven it for ten years and put on about 160,000 miles. We haven't had a car payment in six years. Are we ahead of the cost averages? I believe so.

So what gambits can you use to save money on automobile costs? Here are my suggestions:

1.   Buy a used vehicle and drive it until it falls apart. You save not only on depreciation but also on sales tax, license fee, and insurance.

2.   Consider buying a fleet car or a rental car from a governmental agency.

3.   Consider buying a lease car. At the end of the lease term, normally 3-4 years, these cars may be offered at bargain prices.

4.   Now that interest rates are so low it might benefit you to refinance your existing car loan.

5.   Consider renting a car for specific needs. It could be cheaper to rent if you plan a brief trip of 2,000 miles. What about renting an SUV for weekends in the mountains? New SUVs cost $25,000—$40,000. Should you pay that much if you really need one only a few weekends a year?

6.   I don't have any good suggestions for cutting your repair bills. Modern cars are so technical that you can't do any repairs yourself. I prefer to use the mechanics that operate their own garages as it seems to me the dealerships charge more because they have higher overhead.

Another money saver is to review your bills at the grocery store, restaurant, and other service providers. Too often we find errors that favor the retailer. Advertised discounts are not rung up. Instead you are charged the full price. You can either complain and request a refund or lose. Restaurant bills are often padded, not only by the management, but also by the waitress. One gambit is to ring up the charge twice, if you are paying by credit card. We have also paid the wrong bill—the bill for those in another booth. The waitress kept the overcharge. So always check your monthly credit card bills. Incorrect charges can be removed.

Rebates are another source of savings. Unfortunately too often the rebate is not paid because of some minor technicality. In my opinion it is another form of consumer fraud practiced by large corporations.

Finally protect your image. Don't make yourself a target by ostentatious displays of wealth, or careless behavior. If you're shopping the thrift stores or garage sales it just makes sense to drive your second car, dress conservatively, and not wear a lot of jewelry. Most people believe that others are doing better financially than they are. Therefore if they think you are affluent then they will hit you up for a loan, donation for the church, etc. Also there are others who are looking for an aopportunity to take what you have. Don't leave valuables in your car, either when you park on the street or take your car in for repairs. When leaving your car for repairs don't leave your house keys with the car keys. You don't have to be paranoid, just exercise a reasonable degree of care.

Protecting your assets includes having a Will and setting up a family trust. You may avoid probate expenses and estate taxes. I won't discuss these topics in detail as your local library has numerous books on the subject.

Steps You Can Take Now

The first and most important step, is to refinance your mortgage. Not to do so is crazy, since current interest rates are at their lowest in forty years. My brother just refinanced his rental house. By reducing his interest rate from 7.5% to 5.25% he was able to reduce his monthly payment by $300.00. That's real money. If he had been living in the house as owner-occupant he could have reduced the interest rate further, to 4.75%. In addition he could have avoided the appraisal fee, thus reducing his closing costs by $600.00 or more.

The second step you can take is to postpone buying a new car. As you know the TV waves have been bombarded with car ads. The dealers were offering no interest deals. Two results will flow from this situation. First, we cannot expect vehicle sales in 2003 to be as high. Practically everyone who wanted a new car has just bought one. Therefore where will the new buyers come from? According to *The Wall Street Journal*, November 4, 2002, car sales are already in a slump with October sales of the Detroit Big three manufacturers down 27%. Here is the opportunity , in a year or so, after more job layoffs, those recent car buyers will be dumping their used SUV's for whatever they can get. It will be a buyer's market for those smart enough to wait for the bargains.

The third step you can take is more difficult, and that is to wait. If you have any cash resist the temptation to put it into the stock market because "stocks are low." Instead put it in a money market account or CD because it will take time before the stock market bottoms and then resumes its upward climb. Even though fixed income investments are only paying 2% -3%, that's better than nothing, or even a loss, if you buy back into the stock market too soon. Keep what cash you have available so that when true bargains appear you can pick them up.

Another example, in my opinion, is the overheated bubble in the real estate market. Surely with high unemployment, bankruptcies leading to foreclosures, and lots of vacancies, the resale market for residences is bound to weaken. Keep some cash available and when the time comes, next year, or the year after, pick up some of those bargains at foreclosures.

For those of you still employed you should continue to invest in stocks in your 401K or IRA. At least those of you under age 60 should do so. If you have a minimum of five to ten years until retirement, stocks should have time to recover. Meanwhile, between now and retirement, you will be investing while stocks are cheap. How do you know when stocks are cheap? Just consult Figure 14.

Figure 14: The Correlation of Short-Term Interest Rates and Stock Prices. After Bernstein (1999, Fig. 4-14)

Why You Haven't Felt the Depression Yet

Conditions are different today from the way they were in 1930. At that time the unemployed worker felt the effects immediately. A worker who didn't work had no other source of income. Today we have unemployment insurance, accrued sick leave, social security, health insurance and other benefits. Those workers laid off today typically can draw upon those benefits for six months to a year. Further, many workers laid off may qualify for retirement benefits; albeit at a lower level than they had expected. So the effects of being laid off are dispersed over months or years, rather than being faced all at once.

An additional source of income that may be tapped is savings. Those workers laid off may survive for a while without significant reduction in standard of living as long as their savings hold out.

Even more tempting is to take out a home equity loan. Home prices have escalated dramatically so that a typical homeowner who has owned his home for ten years or more may have an equity of $100,00 to $200,000. Borrowing against that capital gain provides a source of income that many homeowners have tapped.

The primary reason that the true reality of the crash has yet to be felt by the average American is that much of the losses in the stock market were in 401K and other pension accounts. For those workers still employed the losses have not affected their standard of living. It is only their standard of living in the future, after retirement, that will be affected. The problem is that many of those workers will not have sufficient years left in the workforce to recoup those losses. What if the stock market stays flat for the next ten years? What if you continue paying into your 401K but those funds then fail to gain much in value? It could happen. The mortgage broker I met thinks the stock market may not exceed its year 2000 high for at least ten years. The DOW was above 11,000 and the NASDAQ was at 5,000. Today the DOW is 8,400 and the NASDAQ is at 1,300. He could be right in his prediction. Will the NASDAQ be up 450% in the next ten years? Will the DOW be up 50%? Who knows? These are the factors that will shape your future as the Depression unfolds.

The politicians and the press have been talking about "the recovery" for the last year. There isn't any recovery. Their talk is all smoke and mirrors meant to bolster consumer confidence so that everyone will go out and spend money they don't have for things they don't really need. The truth is that the Depression will advance as one factor in a tailspin affects another and another until the whole scenario resembles a row of dominoes toppling against each other.

A Forecast

Economic forecasts are similar to the current U.S. dollar. They are just pieces of paper with ink on them. How well they will hold up in the future is problematic. My forecast for the future of the economy in the next few years isn't any better than anyone else's. However, here goes:

The "recovery" that the politicians and financial gurus promise us is underway will be anemic at best. More likely will be a series of ups and downs that will trend lower over the next year or so. The stock market will finally reach bottom but at a level lower than today. Some stocks will never recover. Their assets will be taken over by creditors in bankruptcy proceedings and stockholders will be left with zilch. Others will be restructured with "reverse splits" and other gambits that will also reduce shareholders' equity.

Job losses will continue to mount as profit margins narrow and globalization continues to shift jobs overseas. The job losses in manufacturing in the third quarter of 2002 were 52,000 in August, 39,000 in September, and 49,000 in October, (The Wall Street Journal, November 4, 2002). That brings the total of unemployed to 8.2 million, 5.7% of the total work force. I believe that total will go even higher. Some jobs will never come back. For example, if your job title was "Information Systems Consultant", forget it. Those jobs are "Gone with the Wind". "Retraining" the often reiterated panacea mentioned by politicians, is probably overstated. It's tempting to think that more education will open up career opportunities but I'm skeptical that it will do so for the majority of job seekers. What it will take to create new jobs is increased demand for manufactured products.

Foreclosures and bankruptcies are already up 50% from a year ago. They will continue to increase. Further, with layoffs, the rental market is already soft with vacancies at 20-year highs. Office and retail space vacancies are twice those in residential rentals. I believe this will intensify and that as a result the bubble in real estate prices will burst. Therefore I anticipate cheaper real estate prices a year from now.

What are the other possibilities? In a time of deflation, real estate values will erode. Stock prices will drop and stagnate. Incomes will fall. It will become harder to service debt. Property taxes however, won't decrease. There will be defaults of corporate bonds. Cash will increase in buying power. The only other assets that will increase in value will be gold and silver and low risk bonds.

Will the government do anything? Probably not much. Unemployment benefits may be extended and some taxes may be reduced, such as the capital gains tax. However the net improvement will be minimal, at least as far as the average American is concerned. The Federal Reserve has already cut interest rates almost as far as possible and that hasn't turned things around. There may not be much the government can do. Owing to the stock market crash, the Bush tax cut, and the war on terrorism, the federal budget experienced a deficit of $159 billion in fiscal 2002 (The Wall street Journal, November 11, 2002). Proposals being considered in Congress include making tax cuts permanent, enacting a prescription drug benefit, eliminating estate taxes and taxes on dividends, and fund a war on Iraq. The total of these, if enacted, could add two trillion dollars to the deficit in the coming decade. Thus federal actions could intensify a depression rather than prevent one. So the economic cycle, in spite of government interference, will run its course.

Will you survive? Probably, but not without stresses and a reduction in your standard of living. However, and this is the good news, once the depression ends inflation will come roaring back. Those who survive the depression will be poised to profit from the ensuing good times.

As to where in the economic cycle we are right now my conclusion is that we are in Stage 7 in Figure 15 below. If that's true then more hard times lie ahead.

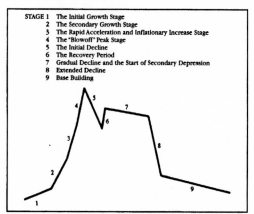

Figure 15: Stages of the Economic Cycle after Bernstein 1999, p. 74

The Doomsday Scenario

What if we enter a major depression? What are the consequences we can expect? In a book titled *Beat the Millennium Crash*, Jake Bernstein (1999) has summarized the bad news as follows:

1.   Banks will fail and account holders will be unable to access their funds.

2.   Businesses will be disrupted and standard consumer goods will be difficult to obtain or even unavailable.

3. Farmers may have difficulty getting their products to market and when there, there may be few buyers as those who have lost their jobs won't have any money.

4. Bankruptcies and foreclosures will rise to astronomical levels.

5. Credit will become severely curtailed.

6. Debt service will become the primary focus of businesses and individuals.

7. Unemployment will soar to the 1930's levels.

Could it get this bad? I don't really think so as the Federal Reserve and the Federal government will apply Keynesian economics to stimulate the money supply and thereby the economy. The government may even go so far as to start a war as a means to stimulate employment. So, in my opinion, storing a year's supply of food, bottled water, ammunition and other survivalist supplies represents an overreaction. Even so, as our historical summaries document, it has happened before.

POSTSCRIPT
WHAT IF YOU DON'T
MAKE IT?

One possibility is that you won't be able to defend yourself in time against the coming depression. What if you lose your job and cannot meet your mortgage payments, then what?

According to *The Wall Street Journal* (November 6, 2002) personal bankruptcies are increasing at an alarming rate. Total bankruptcies in 2001 were 390,064. However in the first two quarters of 2002 the number of new bankruptcies was 400,686. If that rate continues for the rest of the year then the 2002 filings will double those of 2001. That is an ominous trend. The reasons are several; total mortgage debt has increased 50% in the last four years. One in five refinanced their home in the last year, taking advantage of the lower interest rates. However 30% of those borrowed more in order to pay off other debt. Credit card debt is a major contributing factor, up 25% in the last five years. More and more homeowners are tapping their home equity (real wealth) in order to pay current expenses. One result is that 1.2% of all mortgages are now in foreclosure.

How do you know you are in trouble and bankruptcy is in your future? The answer to project your debt payments over the next several years and estimate your future income for that same period. If the debt to income ratio is negative then you are headed into a dark tunnel with no light ahead. At that point bankruptcy becomes a real possibility. However there are options, you still may make choices. Chapter 7 is designed to cancel your personal debts while at the same time it wipes out your assets. Further you cannot obtain any credit for the subsequent 7 years. Chapter 13 permits you to keep your home and some other assets if you restructure your debts and make payments over a 5-year term. It is a court-approved plan, prepared by you, which spells out how you will pay off your creditors. You pay each month the agreed upon payment to a court-appointed trustee who pays the creditors. If you pay the agreed upon amount you retain ownership of your assets.

Under the Federal bankruptcy law debt canceled in a bankruptcy is not included in your taxable income. Further under Chapter 13 the following assets are exempt from claims of your creditors:

Federal Exemptions (Williamson 2001)

1. Residence or burial plot—$16,150.00

2. Household furnishings—$8,650 aggregate, $425.00 max each item

3. Jewelry—$1,075.00

4. Any property selected by debtor—$850.00 plus up to $8,075.00 of unused portion of 1. above.

5. Professional tools—$1,625.00

6. Unmatured life insurance—100%

7. Accrued dividends or interest—$8,625.00

8. Professionally prescribed health aids—100%

9. Social Security and other public annuity benefits—100% of amount necessary for support of debtors and dependents

10.   Alimony—100%

11.   Pensions and annuity payments—100%

12.   Payments on account of bodily injury—$16,150.00

13.   Other payments, crime victim, future earnings, wrongful death, etc—100%

Every state is different. For example, Colorado has a $45,000.00 homestead exemption whereas in Conneticut it is $75,000.00. Other line items differ from federal as well. However these items are exempt only if they are paid for. If they are pledged as collateral against a loan they may be seized and sold. Other potential benefits to you as an employee, embodied in the law, are guaranteed in case your employer goes bankrupt. Up to $2,000 in back wages and fringe benefits are given priority reservations for payment to prior employees, after payments to secured creditors. Such employee claims actually have precedent under the law, over unpaid federal taxes owed by the employer.

Finally if you were a customer of a firm that went bankrupt and had paid for an order in advance, you have priority for a claim of up to $900.00 against that firm's assets. However let's hope that through reliance on a Depression-proof plan you have developed in advance you will come out OK and bankruptcy will not be in your future.

BIBLIOGRAPHY

Allen, Frederick Lewis. "Only Yesterday." *Harpers,* 1931.

Babson, Roger W. *If Inflation Comes, What You Can Do About It.* New York, Frederick A. Stokes, Company, 1941.

Bendiner, Robert. *Just Around the Corner. A highly selective history of the thirties.* New York, Harper and Rowe, 1967.

Bernstein, Jake. *Beat the Millennium Crash.* NY Institute of Finance, 1999.

Broadfoot, Barry. *Ten Lost Years 1929-1939.* Toronto, Doubleday, Canada, Ltd., 1971

Browne, Harry. *How to Profit in the Monetary Crisis.* 1978

Chandler, Lester V. *America's Greatest Depression 1929-1941.* New York, Harper and Rowe, 1970.

Chase, A.W. *Dr. Chase's Recipes or Information for everybody: An invaluable collection of about eight hundred practical recipes.* Ann Arbor, Michigan. Published by the author, 1867.

Committee for Economic Development. *Fighting Inflation and Promoting Growth.* CED, 477 Madison Avenue, N.Y., 1976.

Davis, W.A. *Personal Diary, 1928-1950.* n.d.

English, John Wesley and Gray Emerson Cardiff. *The Coming Real Estate Crash.* Arlington House, 1979.

Erdman, Paul. *The Crash of '79.* Simon and Schuster, 1976.

Flanigan, Patrick. "How safe is your job in a slowdown?" *Money,* pp. 80-81, July 1979.

Freidman, Milton, "Using escalators to help fight inflation." *Fortune,* pp. 94-98, 174-176, July 1974.

Galbraith, John Kenneth. *The Great Crash of 1929.* Boston, Houghton Mifflin, 1955.

A Short History of Financial Euphoria. Whittle Direct Books, 1990.

Galbraith, John Kenneth and Nicole Salinger. *Almost Everyone's Guide to Economics.* Boston, Houghton Mifflin, 1978.

Glickman, Arthur P. *Mr. Badwrench: How you can survive the $20 billion-a year auto repair rip-off.* Seaview Books, N.Y. 1981.

Goldston, Robert. *The Great Depression The United States in the Thirties.* Indianapolis, N.Y., The Bobbs-Merrill Company, Inc., 1968

Hazlett, Henry. *Economics in One Lesson.* New York, MacFadden-Bartell Corporation, 1962.

Hoover, Herbert. *The Memoirs of Herbert Hoover 1929-1941 The Great Depression.* New York, MacMillan, 1952.

Hoppe, Donald, J. *How to Invest in Gold Coins.* New Rochelle, New York, Arlington House, 1970.

Horatio, Algernon. *The Penny Capitalist. How to build a small fortune from next to nothing.* New Rochelle, New York, Arlington House, 1979.

Janeway, Eliot. *What Shall I Do With My Money?* McKay, 1970.

Kelly, Walt. *Pogo's Will Be That Was.* New York, Simon and Schuster, 1979.

Kindleberger, Charles P. *The World in Depression 1929-1939.* London (74 Grosvenor St., London, W1) Allen Lane. The Penguin Press, 1973.

Klein, Roger and William Wolman. *The Beat Inflation Strategy.* New York, Simon and Schuster, 1975.

Klott, Gary. *The Complete Financial Guide to the 1990's.* Times Books, Random House, 1990.

Lasser, J.K. *Your Income Tax.* John Wiley & Sons, N.Y., 2002.

Mandel, Michael. *The Coming Internet Depression.* Basic Books, 2000.

Money Magazine—Fall 2002.

August 2002.

Mooney, F. Bentley. *Creating and Preserving Wealth.* Probus Publishing, Chicago, 1991.

Morgan Stanley, *Perspectives,* October 2002.

Myers, C.V. *The Coming Deflation.* New Rochelle, New York, Arlington House, 1976.

Patterson, Robert T. *The Great Boom and Panic, 1921-1929.* Chicago, Henry Regnery Company, 1965.

Porteus, John. *Coins in History.* New York, G.P. Putnams' Sons, 1969.

Reynolds, John M. "Mineral Wealth from the Sea Floor." *Geographical Magazine,* pp. 21-24, October 1978.

Ruff, Howard. *How to Prosper During the Coming Bad Years.* Times Books, N.Y., 1979.

Schilke, Oscar G. and Raphael E. Solomon. *America's Foreign Coins.* New York, The Coin Currency Institute, Inc. 1964.

Schultz, Harry, D. *Panics and Crashes and How You Can Make Money Out of Them.* New Rochelle, New York, Arlington House, 1972.

172

Stanley, Thomas J. and William D. Danko. *The Millionaire Next Door.* Longstreet Press, Atlanta, 1996.

Temin, Peter. *Did Monetary Forces Cause the Great Depression?* New York, W.W. Norton and Company, Inc., 1976.

Time Magazine. "Inside the big oil game." *Time,* pp. 70-79, May 7, 1979.

October 4, 2002.

October 14, 2002.

Time-Life Editors. *This Fabulous Century,* Vol. IV, 1930-1940. New York, Time-Life Books, 1969.

U.S Congress, Joint Economic Committee. *The Underground Economy: Hearing before the Joint Economic Committee, Congress of the United States, Ninety-sixth Congress, first session, Nov. 15, 1979.* U.S. Government Printing Office, 1980.

Volcker, Paul, A. "The political economy of the dollar." *Quarterly Review,* Federal Reserve Bank of New York, Winter, pp. 1-12, 1979.

Wall Street Journal. October 10, 2002.

November 4, 2002.

November 6, 2002.

November 11, 2002.

White, A.D. "The debtor class." *Harpers,* pp. 39-58. (Originally written 1876) 1979.

Williamson, John H. *Attorneys' Handbook on Consumer Bankruptcy.* Argyle Pubs., Lakewood, CO., 2001.

Wolman, William and Anne Colamosca. *The Judas Economy.* Addison Wesley, 1997.

Printed in the United States
1303300005B/22-69